Purchased with funds from the

Wyoming Community Foundation

McMurry Library Endowment.

"A PUBLIC LIBRARY IS THE NEVER FAILING
SPRING IN THE DESERT." ANDREW CARNEGIE

1910
1970

CARNEGIE LIBRARY

CASPER, WYOMING

A FIELD GUIDE TO

WILDFLOWERS
OF THE
ROCKY
MOUNTAINS

CARL SCHREIER

HOMESTEAD PUBLISHING
Moose, Wyoming

PHOTOGRAPHIC CREDITS

Photography and illustrations by the author, Carl Schreier, unless otherwise noted. Other photography by: Philip Beaurline/Photo-Nats *(Pursh's Milk-vetch 93, Longstalk Clover 101, Big-head Clover 101)*, Willard Clay *(King's Crown 71)*, Bob & Miriam Francis *(Striped Coral Root 39, Common Burdock 179)*, Raymond Gehman *(Wildflower field 10)*, John P. George *(Alpine Laurel 127)*, JM Graphics *(Cushion Coryphantha 113)*, Jessie M. Harris *(Red Lily 31, Spotted Coral Root 37, Ladies-tresses 41, Water Smartweed 43, Ocean-spray 83, Leafy Spurge 105, Poison Ivy 107, Pink Pyrola 131, Marsh Skullcap 153, Yellow Owl-clover 163, Twinflower 171, Alpine Aster 181, Nodding Beggars-tick 183, Broom Snakeweed 195, Stemless Goldenweed 195, White-flowered Hawkweed 199, Prickly Sow-thistle 205)*, Cathy & Gordon Illg *(Groundcherry 155)*, Steven C. Kaufman *(White Dryas 81)*, Jerg Kroener *(Stonecrop 11, Yellow Skunkcabbage 23, Wartberry Fairy-bells 27, Mountain Sorrel 43, Purple Saxifrage 75, Smooth Labrador-tea 129)*, Barbara Magnuson/Photo-Nats *(One-flowered Goldenweed 197)*, Neal & Jane Mishler *(Virgin's Bower 57, Gayfeather 201, Coneflower 201)*, Pat O'Hara *(Showy Milkweed 137)*, R. Pollock *(Canada Violet 111)*, Carl Purcell *(Missouri Goldenrod 205)*, Steve Solum *(Watercress 67, Deer Horn 115)*, Neena Wilmot *(Mockorange 77, Field Mint 151)*.

Cover photograph: Parry's Primrose

Copyright © 1996 by Carl Schreier. Second edition, 2002.
All rights reserved. No part of this book may be reproduced or transmitted in any form or by any means, electronic or mechanical, including photocopying, recording, or by any other information storage and retrieval system, without written permission from the publisher.
ISBN 0-943972-13-2
Library of Congress Catalog Card Number 89-81183
Printed in Hong Kong.

Published by
HOMESTEAD PUBLISHING
Box 193, Moose, Wyoming 83012
Denver, CO & San Francisco, CA

For a complete listing of other natural history publications
from Homestead Publishing, please send for a catalog.

CONTENTS

WILDFLOWERS
of the
ROCKY MOUNTAINS

Nowhere else on Earth is there a richer variety and array of wildflowers than along the cordillera called the Rocky Mountains, which spans the length of the North American continent. The Rockies extend more than 3,000 miles and are composed of a series of ranges beginning at the semiarid slopes of the Sangre de Cristo Mountains in central New Mexico and reaching to the cold and treeless region of the Brooks Range in northwest Alaska. They are defined by the western edge of the Great Plains on the east and by a series of broad basins and plateaus on the west. A centerline called the Continental Divide winds along the backbone of these mountain ranges and separates west-flowing streams, those flowing to the Pacific Ocean, from east-flowing streams, those flowing to the Atlantic or Arctic ocean. Many prominent peaks are found along this spine of the Continental Divide. The highest peak in the Rockies, Mt. Elbert (el. 14,433 feet/4,399

The Rocky Mountain system of North America extends nearly 3,000 miles (4,800 km) from New Mexico to northwestern Alaska, and from the intercoastal ranges to the Great Plains.

meters), is in Colorado. Mt. Robson, (el. 12,972 feet/3,954 meters), dominates the Canadian Rockies.

Geologically, the Rocky Mountains are composed of folded mountains or belts that run north-south. The ranges comprising the Rockies were formed individually or in groups during the Cordilleran orogeny of the Mesozoic Era (230 million to 63 million years ago). The Rockies then underwent further reforming, modifying and exposing as a result of a geologically complex system of uplifts—the prominent mountain-building process occurring as a series of pulses during this period. Erosion—which exposed crystalline cores and thick layers of sedimentary rock—and volcanism, which added ash layers and helped in the soil-building process, also played roles, along with glaciation—the scouring and transportation process.

The Rockies have formed a natural barrier—an island on the North American Continent—and, since glacial times, plants have colonized, survived, reproduced and adapted to a new environment. As a consequence, slightly different species have evolved here than on neighboring regions. Penstemons (above), as a group, have evolved a diverse range of sizes, shapes and colors along the cordillera.

Since the last glacial epoch, which began nearly 250,000 years ago and ended when the most recent ice sheets receded 12,000 to 15,000 years ago, the flora of the Rocky Mountains and the upper Northern Hemisphere recolonized and reestablished. With the retreating glaciers, plants invaded from warmer, southern climes and adapted to a changing environment. As a result, circumpolar or circumboreal plants—generally found continuously across arctic/alpine or subarctic North America, Greenland, northern Europe and northern Asia—evolved in a relatively short span of time. The dandelion is an example of a widespread and highly success-ful postglacial species. Other species became isolated by topography, soil and climate and evolved into unique and often rare species, such as members of the orchid family.

The geographical expanse of the Rocky Mountains is so immense that the Rockies often are broken into five topo-graphical sections: the Southern, Middle and Northern Rockies of the continental United States; the Rocky Mountain system of Canada; and the Brooks Range in Alaska. The contrast in climate, temperature, elevation and daylight from the southern end to the northern end of the chain is extreme. The flowering season in the Southern Rockies may begin as early as March and end as late as October. During this period, there is an average of 12 to 15 hours of daylight during a summer day. And yet, at the other extreme in Canada and northern Alaska, the flower season does not start until mid-May and ends by mid-August. During this period, 24 hours of daylight occur from mid-June to mid-August. This continuous daylight, even with a short growing season, allows plants to grow, flower and seed just as their southern coun-terparts do. Similarly, temperature variations can be extreme. On the Canadian border, halfway along the Rockies, the greatest tem-perature change ever recorded in a single day happened on January 23, 1916. On that day, the temperature changed 100° F, drop-ping from 44° F above zero to 56° F below zero.

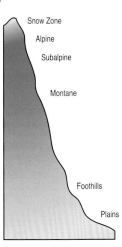

Snow Zone

Alpine

Subalpine

Montane

Foothills

Plains

Temperature and precipitation are among the most important aspects of climate, and it is changes in these that, ventur-ing up a mountainside or trav-eling north, produces the strik-ingly similar sequence of natu-ral vegetation zones. This change is roughly equivalent to a rise of 1,000 feet on a mountainside or moving 100 miles farther north.

The natural plant communi-ties associated with the Rocky Mountains begin with the plains or grassland zone, the foothills zone, the montane zone, the subalpine zone, and the alpine zone, and the high-est is the permanent snow zone, where only simple or-ganisms can live.

Even with such fluctuations of sunlight and temperature, some things remain constant. High altitude and high latitude have almost the same effect on plant growth. In the Southern Rockies, treeline begins at about 11,500 feet; at the Canadian border, it is near 7,500 feet, while in the Brooks Range, treeline begins at about sea level. Drawing a line at those eleva-tions produces a demarcation called a vegetation zone. At treeline (also called elfin wood or krummholz, a German word meaning "crummy wood"), most trees are gnarled and twisted. Above treeline, full-sized trees cannot grow. This demarcation also denotes the be-ginning of the *alpine* or *tundra zone*. Below treeline, beginning with the lowest zone, are the *plains* or *grassland zone*, the *foothill* or *shrub zone*, the *montane zone*, and the *subal-pine zone*. These vegetation zones remain fairly constant along the entire length of the Rockies, with only minor changes in species and floral composition.

The *plains* or *grassland zone* is the lowest and usually the driest and windiest of the habitat zones. It is character-ized by extensive, level or undulating, treeless regions dominated by perennial grasses or sedges, including wheat and bunch grasses. This zone is mainly represented by the Great Plains along the eastern base of the Rocky Mountains and by the intercoastal plains, including the Great Basin, along the western flank. The *grassland zone* reaches into the Rockies proper as fingers along valley bottoms and up warmer, drier south-facing slopes, influencing and enriching the Rocky Mountain flora. This zone also is marked by reduced precipitation as a result of prevailing west-to-east weather patterns. Moisture-laden clouds that form over the Pacific Ocean cool, condense and drop their loads as rain or snow in the higher mountain elevations of the intercoastal ranges and the Rocky Mountains. A rain shadow is formed east of the mountain ranges, where annual precipitation can average as little as eight to 12 inches a year in the north.

The size, extent and topography of the Rockies has led to a variety and diversity of angiosperms, or flowering plants.

The *foothill* or *shrub zone* extends along the Rocky Mountains where the plains break into rug-ged escarpments. It is characterized by rolling, grassy foot-hills, alluvial fans, and brush coulees. This zone has a slight de-crease in temperature and an increase in precipitation. As a general rule, tempera-ture drops about three degrees Fahrenheit per 1,000-foot increase of elevation. Precipitation usually increases propor-tionally with altitude, depending upon topography and the rain-shadow effect. Correspondingly, there is a change in vegetation. In the Southern Rockies, the foothill zone is one of open, shrubby expanses of sagebrush, juniper, mountain mahogany, piñon pine or shrub-oak. Farther north, it is dominated by fescue grassland, sedges, chokecherry, servi-ceberry or willow thickets. The upper limit of this zone is marked by a transition to ponderosa pine in the southern region and lodgepole pine in the north.

The *montane zone* is characterized by the beginning of the mountain forests; montane actually means growing or inhabiting the mountains. Its lower limit is defined by the piñon-juniper belt in the Southern, Middle and Northern Rockies. These tree species appear stunted, deformed or shrubby at their high altitudinal limit of 8,000 feet in New Mexico or 4,000 feet in Montana. In the southern region of the Rocky Mountains, ponderosa pine is the dominant species of the montane zone. Ponderosa pine typically clusters together and forms parklike openings and meadows. A transition in dominant species occurs in the Middle Rockies northward, especially along the western slopes of the Continental Divide, where Douglas fir predominates. An intermingling of Douglas fir and lodgepole pine also occurs in this region. Farther north, lodgepole pine—especially on drier sites—becomes the dominant species.

The *subalpine zone* is perhaps the most luxuriant of the vegetation zones. It commonly receives more precipitation than the lower zones, and winter snow accumulation slowly releases moisture through the shorter summer growing season. A continuous source of moisture allows this zone to support a heavier coniferous growth, forming a dense closed-canopy forest. This zone typically is represented by Engelmann spruce and subalpine fir. Five-needle pines—limber, bristlecone and whitebark—also are intermingled in the *subalpine zone*.

The evolution of flowering plants is, in large part, the specialized relationships between flowers and their insect pollinators. Flies (above), not bees, are the chief pollinators of high-elevation Rocky Mountain flowers. Some flowers, such as sticky geranium (below), have developed "nectary guides" at the base of the corolla to signal pollinating insects, but when the flower has been pollinated, the guides fade.

The highest vegetation zone is the *alpine* or *tundra zone*. It is the treeless region above treeline, or krummholz. It supports a rich growth of wildflowers on a thick sod of grasses and sedges. The terrain generally is rocky or gravelly, with sparse soil, level to steep slopes, and exposed windswept ridges. Tundra refers to arctic regions that usually have a permanently

frozen subsoil, blanketed with a thick turf of low-growing vegetation such as lichens, mosses, tussock grasses and stunted shrubs. This zone receives the most precipitation, 30 inches or more a year. But it is colder, has a shorter growing season with longer, harsher winters, and—in the higher elevations on exposed mountain ridges and peaks—it is windswept and barren with sparse vegetation. Flowers bloom in the alpine or tundra zone during the longest days of the summer—mid-June to mid-

Stonecrops are found primarily on windswept ridges, resembling desert environments. Special water-storing tissue conserves water from dessicating winds.

Asa Gray (top), a re-nowned botanist, spent his career at Harvard studying and cataloging dried speci-mens that arrived by com-missioned explorers. But at the age of 67, Gray made his first journey west to collect for himself.

Thomas Nuttall (middle) became the pre-eminent naturalist who won the West.

John M. Coulter, at age 20, accompanied F.V. Hay-den in his Rocky Mountain explorations during 1872-73 and later wrote the first Western botanical manual.

July—at the peak flowering season and summer solstice in the Rocky Mountains.

The extremes in growing conditions, charac-terized by low precipitation, desiccating winds, abundant sunlight and fluctuating temperatures, have prompted the flora of the Rockies to evolve adaptations to cope. The major adaptation, for either a plains species or an alpine species, is the reduction of water to evaporation from plant tis-sues. This reduction has been accomplished in a number of ways. Water loss can be reduced by having a waxy surface like those on cactuses or kinnikinnik. Some plants developed special sto-mata—minute pores on the surface of the leaf that allow carbon dioxide to enter and water vapor to escape for photosynthesis—which open at night during cooler temperatures rather than during midday heat. Stonecrops have developed this mechanism. Others possess a dense pubes-cence—a tangle of long hairs that reduce wind evaporation and act as a sunscreen, filtering out harmful solar radiation and intense light.

Alpine flora have evolved other adaptations to an extreme and harsh growing environment as well. Because of the short growing season, most plants are perennials, allowing them to resprout, flower, seed and complete their life cycles during a short season. Many display a relatively large flower size, yet possess dwarf vegetative parts that grow close to the ground as mats or stunted growths because of strong winds. Alpine plants also must be hardy enough to withstand freezing conditions, even during flowering seasons.

Yet another influence affecting establishment and growth of mountain flora is aspect. The align-ment or exposure of a mountain to the sun greatly influences the type of vegetation that grows there. A southern exposure, whereby the sun's rays warm and dry the slope, sheds its snow cover earlier than its northern counterpart. There, snow-pack remains into the summer, slowly releasing moisture to feed aquifers and perennial streams. A southern exposure thus limits the type of plant that can establish and explains why grassland can exist on one side of a ridge and a dense forest on the other. This phenomenon—two entirely different habitats, side by side, contrasting with the climate of the area—is called microclimate.

Extremes in latitude, altitude, geology and soils, topography, precipitation and temperature have created an environment suitable for the evolution and establishment of a rich variety of Rocky Mountain angiosperms, or flowering plants. When the first botanical explorers entered the Rocky Mountain region, they discovered the uniqueness of the flora. The Lewis and Clark expedition (1804-1806) conducted the first major scientific study of the Rocky Mountains. Its discoveries of new species, like the bitterroot, and the extensive collections, later analyzed by Frederick Pursh in 1808, established the first descriptive flora for this region. Subsequent investigators include Edwin James, a surgeon and naturalist of the Stephen Long Expedition (1820), who sent his collections to John Torrey. The 1825-1832 discoveries of Northwest explorer-botanist David Douglas and the 1833 explorations of Boston businessman Nathaniel J. Wyeth both sent their collections to Thomas Nuttall. The explorer John Charles Fremont, during his 1845-1848 journeys, also sent his collections to Torrey. These early explorers all contributed to the initial knowledge of Rocky Mountain flora.

The simple tools that botanist Asa Gray used during his Western collecting trip include a vasculum, or plant box (top), a knife and trowel (center), and hand-held and mounted magnifying glasses (bottom).

Three botanists—Thomas Nuttall (1786-1859) of Harvard College, John Torrey (1796-1873) of Columbia College, and his student, Asa Gray (1810-1888), who became a professor of botany at Harvard—systematically began to describe specimens received from the Rocky Mountain explorers. They meticulously cataloged the wealth of new information, of new genera and species collected from a distant region. In turn, they were overwhelmed with the variety and diversity of Rocky Mountain flora. All three eventually journeyed to the Rockies, recorded their own discoveries and expanded the previous knowledge base. They became the pioneers of the study of Rocky Mountain flora.

John Coulter collected specimens from many of the high summits of Colorado, Wyoming, Montana and Idaho. These collections became the basis for the first Manual of Botany of the Rocky Mountain Region.

The trailblazers began the westward expansion and opened new routes, trails and tracks into the rugged terrain of the Rockies, which later led to easier access. These routes allowed other, more refined, explorers to venture into the Rockies in style. Sir William Drummond Stewart, a wealthy Scottish explorer, encouraged four botanists to accompany him on a luxurious scientific exploration (1834) into the Rocky Mountains. Of the four, Austrian Karl Geyer made the greatest contribution. He traveled extensively through the West collecting specimens, which later were sold in England at £2 for 100 specimens.

During the mid- to late 19th century, Europe—especially England—had the greatest influence on botanical exploration, identification and specimen naming. Joseph Burke (1812-1873) was one of these English influences. He traveled along the Oregon Trail into the Rocky Mountains, documenting flora. His specimens now reside at the Royal Botanic Garden, Kew, Surrey, England. During this period, two English botanists, George

Bentham (1800-1884) and Joseph Hooker (1817-1911), also journeyed to the Rockies. Both men described and named numerous specimens. Their common and scientific names still apply to native flora.

By the end of the nineteenth century, Rocky Mountain flora collections were extensive and compilation of this material began. The first to write a

Sticky geranium (Geranium viscosissimum), a common and colorful Rocky Mountain wildflower, belongs to a large group of flowering plants called angiosperms.

book about Rocky Mountain flora was John Merle Coulter (1851-1928). He first came to the Rockies as a 20-year-old official botanist of the 1871 U.S. Geological Survey, lead by Ferdinand Hayden into the Yellowstone country. Coulter later became a professor at the University of Chicago and was the first to compile this information into the *Manual of Botany of the Rocky Mountain Region* (1885). Revised by Aven Nelson in 1909, Coulter's manual contained descriptions of 2,733 species, largely the flora of the northern Rockies. In 1917, Per Axel Rydberg (1860-1931) of the New York Botanical Gardens published his book, *Flora of the Rocky Mountains and Adjacent Plains.* It was the first publication to cover the Rocky Mountains from northern New Mexico to southern Canada. It contained an astonishing 5,900 species. Today, it is believed that between 12,000 and 15,000 plant species exist in the western states and Canada.

In describing, organizing and classifying flora, the first Rocky Mountain botanists used a system of taxonomy that was developed by ancient Greeks. The Greeks used a crude system to divide plants into three main categories. A plant was either a tree, a shrub or an herb. The father of modern plant taxonomy, Swedish botanist Carolus Linnæus (1707-1778), refined the system and systematically began to name and classify plants during the late eighteenth century. He made order from confusion. Plants with widespread distribution through Europe had different common names, depending upon their geographic location, the language of the region and the historical folklore of the area. One species could have several—even hundreds—of common names; there was not a universal standard name for a German to communicate with an Italian and refer to the same species. Linnæus devised a system of binomial nomenclature—a classification consisting of two names—based on Latin, which was

Rocky Mountain iris (Iris missouriensis) *belongs to the* Iridaceae Family, *distinguished by floral parts in series of threes; a racemose inflorescence; long, narrow equitant leaves; and a rhizomatous root system.*

the popular language of scholars of the time and was not partial to any particular language or country.

Linnæus' system uses scientific names, the first representing the genus or family group and the second the species that identifies each unique plant. The first name, or generic name, represents the family association; thus, the scientific name *Geranium viscosissimum* denotes that it is a member of the family Geraniaceae. The last name, or specific name, usually refers to a particular feature of the plant, the location in which it was discovered, or the botanist who first described it. In this example, *viscosissimum* is a Latin derivative and means "very sticky" because the foliage, stems and buds of this plant are sticky to the touch. This scientific name also is reflected in the common name, sticky geranium.

Lilies have their floral parts in multiples of threes, but usually with regular flowers in which the sepals (calyx) and petals (corolla) are similar in appearance.

The Geranium family, in turn, belongs to a class named Magnoliopsida (dicotyledons—plants characterized by a pair of embryonic seed leaves that appear at germination). Plants within this class have basic and common similarities but not enough to separate them into individuals. This class, in turn, belongs to a division

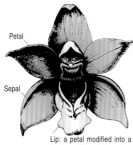

Petal

Sepal

Lip: a petal modified into a landing platform for insects.

Members of the Orchid Family *represent the most specialized flowers of the monocots.*

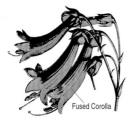

Fused Corolla

Figworts usually have opposite leaves and irregular, bilabiate, tubular corollas.

Disk Flower   Ray Flower

Receptacle

Involucral Bracts

Stigma

Fused anthers

Corolla

Pappus Scale
(modified sepal)

Members of the largest and most complex family, the composites or Asteraceae, *are comprised of flower heads (top). Each flower head is composed of tiny disk flowers—sometimes several hundred—that produce a single seed, whereas the outside ring of showy ray flowers usually is completely sterile. Together, these composites have the appearance of a single, large flower.*

named Magnoliophyta. These are vascular plants with a specialized system for movement of water, minerals and sugars. The first and highest classification in which all plants belong is called the Kingdom Plantae. The Plant Kingdom is a lumping of all plants and does not differentiate between a sticky geranium or a lodgepole pine. The scope of this book covers two main classes of flowering plants: the Magnoliopsida (dicots) and the Liliopsida (monocots—plants with single embryonic seed leafs that appear at germination, such as orchids and lilies).

Wildflowers in this field guide are arranged by families—groups with similar features and structure—and follow an evolutionary order. This guide uses the same manner of floristic manuals and begins with the simplest flowering plants—monocots (lilies for example), and moves to more complex, multiflowered dicots (such as composites). Within this organization, flowering plants are grouped first within the family to which they belong and, secondly within their proper genus. Genera are arranged within each family alphabetically. Thus, a red monkey flower is located under the Figwort Family (Scrophulariaceae) and alphabetically under *Mimulus*.

The system of arranging flowers by colors is not used here because of the wide variation of color. Hood's phlox *(Phlox hoodii),* for example, first appears as a white blossom and turns pink or blue as it matures and fades. So is this species a white, pink, or blue flower? Instead, the grouping of very similar flowers, or members of closely related groups—species, genera and families—aids in understanding and identifying flowers. In this book, 52 families are covered, and many of the basic and common species belong to just a few of these families. Learning the basic family characteristics of these common groups will provide a general familiarity with wildflowers throughout the Rocky

Mountains. Knowing the general characteristics of these families, including the Lily, Buttercup, Rose, Mint, Pea and Sunflower families, will ease the confusion of differentiating one species from a thousand or more species within a full color spectrum.

Each family has several characteristics that identify it. The main characteristics to look for in a flower are shape and structure—how the flowers and leaves are arranged, the number of flower parts, sepals, petals, stamens and ovaries. Also look at the symmetry of a flower. When you draw an imaginary line vertically through a flower, does it produce two mirror images or two different lopsided images? The fusion of floral parts, whereby similar flower parts fuse together to form one unit like a trumpet- or funnel-shaped flower, and whether the flower is superior or inferior, also are good distinguishing indicators. The flower is *superior* when the ovary is in the center of the flower with all the other parts attached to its base. It is *inferior* when the flower parts are attached at the top of the ovary.

Members of the Lily Family (Liliaceae) have parts in threes: three sepals—which may look like petals in some species, give the appearance of six petals; three petals; six stamens; and an ovary with three chambers. Members of the Buttercup Family (Ranunculaceae) have simple structures in which the sepals and petals are separate and distinct, not fused, with numerous stamens and many separate ovaries. While the Rose Family (Rosaceae) has similar features, it is distinguished by the fact that the bases of the sepals, petals and stamens join to form a cup, or hypanthium, around the ovary or ovaries. Members of the Mint Family (Lamiaceae, once called Labiatae) are distinguished by their four-sided, square stems, opposite leaves, minty aroma and technical features of two or four stamens, plus an ovary that is divided into four hard segments, or nutlets. Members of the Pea Family (Fabaceae, once called Leguminosae) are easy to recognize by their distinctive, irregular corollas. These corollas are comprised of five united petals forming a banner, two wings and two lower petals joined to form the keel, plus one pistil that develops into a single-celled pod called a legume. The most complex group is the Sunflower or Composite Family (Asteraceae, once called Compositae). This large group offers the most difficulty when distinguishing individual members. What appears to be a single flower actually is a composite of hundreds of individual flowers. Forming the outside ring on a typical sunflower are ray flowers, and the inner cluster consists of disk flowers. Each individual disk flower bears an inferior ovary that produces a single seed.

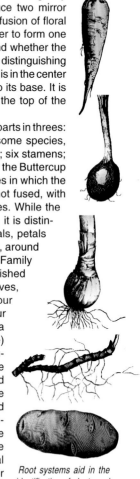

Root systems aid in the identification of plants and help determine if a plant is an annual, biannual or a perennial. The common types are (from top to bottom) fibrous, tap, corm, bulb, rhizome and tuber.

A key in the back of this book aids in distinguishing families and gives the characteristics of each. When you identify a plant family, the next step is to determine the genus, grouped under families. Again, these will have similar and more defined characteristics. Determining the genus of a species may be more than adequate because it might be difficult to determine individual species in some instances. Many groups or genera, especially in the pea family, are difficult to identify to species without knowing the minute technical features or finding the plant in the appropriate flowering or seed stage. Determining the correct group or genus usually is sufficient in identifying a flower in the field.

In helping to identify a flower, look for distinguishing characteristics, such as the habitat in which the flower is found; the type of root system; plant size, stem structure; leaf arrangement and shape; flowering arrangement or type of inflorescence; color, numbers and arrangement of sepals, petals and other floral parts; and the type of fruit it produces.

Roots are the fundamental anchoring system and the means through which water and nutrients are absorbed and sometimes stored. A root also can help determine whether a plant is an annual or perennial. Plants with *fibrous roots* generally are annuals, especially those with less-extensive root systems. Fibrous roots also tend to be irregularly branched.

Taproots tend to have a main, stout axis extending vertically, and often bear smaller lateral roots. This central axis often can be thickened by storage of food. A carrot is an example of a taproot. Many annuals and biennials and some perennials have this type of root system.

More specialized root systems include *corms, bulbs, rhizomes* and *tubers*. All these are underground modified stems that serve as food storage and often aid in reproduction.

The *stem* is the axis of the plant from which all other parts arise. Along the stem are joints, called *nodes* (the space between nodes are called internodes), and from these branches, leaves and sometimes roots grow as buds. If there is only one leaf to a node, it is arranged *alternately* on the

Types of leaf shapes and margins include (from top to bottom): lanceolate, linear, ovate, spatulate, heart-shaped, round, serrate-edged, and lobed.

stem. If there are two leaves at each node, they are arranged *oppositely* on the stem. And if there are more than three leaves to a node, they are arranged in *whorls*. The angle formed by the stem and leaf stalk is called the *axil*, and buds formed in the axils are called *axillary buds*.

A leaf can be an important aid in identifying a flower. Each leaf consists of a *stalk* (petiole), a *blade*, and sometimes *stipules*, or winglike append-ages at the base of certain leaves. In some instances, the petiole is absent and the leaf then is *sessile* on the stem. Leaves can be either simple or compound. For a *simple leaf*, the blade consists of a single piece. A *compound leaf* is composed of many small *leaflets*, arranged either *pinnately* along a central stalk, or attached at the end of a stalk that spread *palmately* like fingers. Leaflets never have axillary buds, but compound leaves always have one at the base. Leaves growing at ground level and appearing to rise from one source are called *basal* leaves and often form a cluster, or *rosette*.

Leaves and leaflets come in a variety of shapes and forms. The most common outlines or shapes of a blade are *lanceolate* (shaped like the tip of a lance), *ovate* (egg-shaped, with a pointed tip), *linear* (line-shaped), *spatulate* (spatula-shaped), *heart-shaped, arrow-shaped* or *round.* Some descriptions will have the Greek prefix *ob-* attached to it, describing that it is in a reverse direction. In addition, leaf mar-gins or edges can be *smooth*, or *entire*, *scalloped, serrate, deeply lobed, toothed*, or even double toothed.

Another distinguishing feature for leaves is the type of venation. Most monocots, such as grasses and lilies, have *parallel venation*, in which the veins, or vascular ridge on a leaf, extend the length of the leaf and parallel each other and the leaf margin. Dicots, on the other hand, have *netted venation*, whereby veins branch and form a netted pattern. Most palmately lobed leaves are *palmately veined*, a pattern like the fingers on a hand.

The flowering cluster or its arrangement on the axis is called the *inflorescence*. If only one flower appears at the end of a stalk, it is called a *solitary* inflorescence. If the plant is unbranched and the flowers appear to lack flower stalks (pedicels), it is a *spike;* the

Margin

Petiole

Leaflets

Types of leaves include (from top to bottom): simple, compound, palmately compound, pinnately compound and rosette.

white bog-orchid is a good example. If the flowers have stalks, it is a *raceme*, the most common form of inflorescence. If the raceme is irregularly or alternately branched, it is a *panicle*. If it is oppositely and regularly branched, it is a *cyme*. If all the flower stalks (pedicels) arise form one point and are equal in length, it forms an *umbel*, and multiple branching forms a compound umbel, such as cow parsnip. But if the flower stalks arise from different positions on the axis and are different lengths but arrive at the same level and appear flat-topped, it is a *corymb*. In the case of the Sunflower Family (Asteraceae), a cluster of numerous, tiny flowers form a button-like *head*. A head generally is composed of two types of flowers—the outside ring of usually colorful *ligules* or *ray flowers* and the inner *tubular* or *disk flowers*.

Most flowers consist of four series of parts. The outside series or ring usually is green, but in lilies, this series may be colored, is called the *calyx*, and is comprised of *sepals*. Within the calyx is the *corolla*, comprised of the highly colorful and showy *petals*. The terms calyx and corolla generally are used when they are united, forming bell- or funnel-shaped flowers. The calyx and corolla together are called the *perianth*. The next series just inside the petals are *stamens*. Each stamen consists of a relatively slender stalk, called the *filament*, tipped with a pollen-bearing *anther*. The stamens can be either separate, united to each other, or fused to other floral parts.

In the very center of the flower, or the innermost series, is one or more pistils. The *pistil* can be either simple or compound and is composed of a swollen base, the *ovary*, a slender, sometimes branched *style*, topped with a *stigma*, which receives pollen. Inside the ovary are *ovules* that, when fertilized, develop into seeds. A *carpel* is a structure of the pistil and is said to be compound if it is composed of two or more united carpels. Ovules usually are borne along the margins of a carpel.

After the ovules have been fertilized, the ovary and other parts associated with it begin to ripen into a *fruit* to aid in distribution of seeds. The most common form is a hardcased, one-seeded fruit called an *achene*. Most members of the Sunflower Family produce achenes. Another type of dry fruit is a *dry capsule*, produced by some members of the lilies and as follicles in columbines.

Fleshy fruits are derived from various structures of the flower. A *pome* represents a fruit in which the calyx enlarges and encloses the ovary; apples and

Types of inflorescences include (from top to bottom): solitary, spike, raceme, panicle, corymb, umbel and compound umbel.

serviceberries are examples. Other fleshy fruits include strawberries, in which the receptacle enlarges and each ovary has an achene attached to it. A fruit in which the outer seed coat becomes fleshy is called a *drupe;* plums are an example. It is typical of raspberries for clusters of small drupes, called *drupelets*, to attach to the receptacle but separate when ripe. True *berries* are soft fruits with seeds embedded in the pulp, like huckleberries.

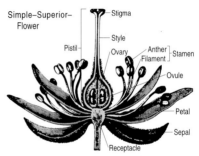

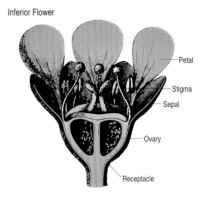

Various types of dicots have different positions of the ovary. Superior ovaries (top) have floral parts attached below the ovaries; their flowers are perigynous. Conversely, the floral parts are attached above inferior ovaries; their flowers are epigynous.

Aurum Family
Araceae

YELLOW SKUNK CABBAGE   *Lysichitum americanum*

This large herbaceous perennial can have leaves that grow up to five feet in height. It is recognizable by a conspicuous eight- to 20-inch flowering stalk with a corncob-like spike of small, crowded, yellow or greenish flowers surrounded by a bright yellow bract called a spathe. HABITAT/RANGE: Yellow skunk cabbage prefers open swamps and wet woods in lowlands from Alaska to central California and east to the western slopes of the Rocky Mountains. Blooms during April to early July. FACTS/USES: The common name refers to the fetid odor produced by the plant to attract flies for pollination. The root is edible after roasting or drying, and Native Americans were known to grind it into flour. Eaten raw, this plant produces a stinging or burning sensation in the mouth. Cooking or drying breaks or releases calcium oxalate, the noxious compound, so that it can be eaten without ill effects.

Lily Family
Liliacea

NODDING ONION   *Allium cernuum*

Nodding onion is a perennial herb with a characteristic onion or garlic odor and taste. It grows six to 18 inches tall on slender, erect stalks from elongated, layered bulbs. The small, white or pinkish flowers are clustered in an umbel that droops or nods at the end of the stalk. The leaves, mostly basal, are long and somewhat grasslike. HABITAT/RANGE: This species is one of the most common wild onions found in North America. It prefers moist sites of valleys, open hillsides to mountain meadows. It is distributed across southern Canada from British Columbia to New York, south to Georgia, Wisconsin, Texas, Mexico and southern Oregon. Flowers during June to August. FACTS/USES: Allium is the ancient Latin name for garlic. The specific name, *cernuum*, means drooping or nodding. In the spring, wildlife feed upon the bulbs and foliage, and when dairy cows graze on onion, it flavors the milk they produce.

TEXTILE ONION   *Allium textile*

Textile onion is a slender perennial that ascends and reproduces by bulbs, aerial bulblets or seed. The three- to 15-inch unbranched, leafless, round stalk terminates in an open umbel of 15 or more flowers. Each flower is comprised of six white or pinkish tepals and six stamens, attached by a long pedicel. Each stalk, rising from a clump, has two long, roundish, basal leaves. The stalks and leaves have an onion or garlic odor. HABITAT/RANGE: A plant of plains and foothills of Idaho to Alberta, Manitoba, Minnesota and south to New Mexico and Utah. Flowers in early summer. FACTS/USES: The Latin specific name, *textile*, refers to the net-like coat of fibers covering the bulb. All the onions are edible and can be prepared a number of ways. The bulbs can be eaten raw, cooked or boiled. The leaves, too, can be used as seasoning. Consuming large quantities of onion, like many native foods, can cause poisoning.

DOUGLAS' BRODIAEA   *Brodiaea douglasii*

This flower has an onion-like appearance. Five to 15 blue tubular flowers are clustered in a terminal umbel. Each one-inch, tubular flower is comprised of six fused tepals with flared lobes, and each flower is attached by a short pedicel. The one- to three-foot, erect, leafless stalks ascend from bulb-like corms. The narrow, grasslike leaves are basal and seldom exceed the height of the flowering stalk. HABITAT/RANGE: Douglas' brodiaea inhabits well-drained slopes of grasslands and sagebrush plains to pine and montane forests. It is distributed from British Columbia to Montana, south to Utah and northern California. Flowers from late April to mid-July. FACTS/USES: The generic name honors the Scottish botanist, James Brodie, and the specific name honors the Northwest explorer-botanist, David Douglas. The edible corms were used by Native Americans and early pioneers, who ate them raw or cooked.

SEGO LILY   *Calochortus gunnisonii*

The sego lily is a goblet-like perennial flower with three narrow, greenish sepals and three broad, cream-colored petals with an elongated, often fringe-margined gland near the base. The long, narrow basal leaves are channeled and V-shaped in cross section. Each tall, slender stem, six to 18 inches high, terminates in a single flower. HABITAT/RANGE: An inhabitant of meadows to light woods, this Rocky Mountain species is common east of the Continental Divide, from central Montana to South Dakota, south to New Mexico, eastern Arizona and Utah. Blooms from May to mid-July. FACTS/USES: Another common name for sego lily is *mariposa lily*, a Spanish word meaning butterfly. The Greek generic name, *Calochortus*, is a derivative of *kalo*, meaning beautiful, and *chortos*, meaning grass. Although most sego lilies reproduce from seeds, it takes three to five years for seedlings to establish bulbs and flower.

NUTTALL'S SEGO LILY   *Calochortus nuttallii*

This erect, slender-stemmed perennial herb has a terminal, white, wineglass-shaped flower. Each flower has three lanceolate, greenish sepals and three triangular-shaped petals. At the base of each petal is a roundish gland, fringed with hairs, and an arched brownish-purple spot above the gland. The pale green leaves are slender and grasslike. HABITAT/RANGE: Prefers dry, grassy or open sagebrush foothills of the Rocky Mountains, from Oregon, Montana and North Dakota to New Mexico and California. An early summer bloomer. FACTS/USES: This is Utah's state flower and commemorates the 1847 arrival of Brigham Young and his followers into the Salt Lake valley. The first few years, they faced famine caused by drought, cricket infestations, and heavy frosts. The sweet, starchy bulb-like roots of the sego lily helped sustain the pioneers through those harsh times.

COMMON CAMAS *Camassia quamash*

Common camas is a perennial, bulbous herb that grows one to two feet high. The bright blue to purplish flowers are arranged in loose racemes. The six tepals (sepals and petals are similar) spread outward in a star pattern with six yellow stamens. Most of the long, linear leaves are basal, with a few leaflike bracts in the inflorescence. HABITAT/RANGE: Camas prefers moist or wet meadows that often dry by late spring. It is found from British Columbia to Alberta, south to Colorado and California. When it flowers in early spring, camas produces large fields of blue that, from a distance, resemble pools of water. FACTS/USES: Camas has been one of the most significant staples and monetary plants of Western Indians. The bulbs are dug in spring but care must be taken not to collect death camas (*Zigadenus venenosus*). Camas bulbs are either cooked, producing a sweet gummy taste, or dried for later use.

BEADLILY *Clintonia uniflora*

This low-growing perennial herb usually has one distinct white flower terminating on a three- to eight-inch slender stalk. Six tepals flare back into a star shape, revealing six yellow stamens. The two to three leaves are mostly basal, broad and bright green. After the flower matures, it develops into a blue berry. The extensive rhizomatous root system produces a number of paired leaves surrounding the flowering plant. HABITAT/RANGE: This dweller of moist or wet soils in shaded coniferous forests is found from foothills to montane forests. It is distributed from Alaska to California, but mainly west of the Rocky Mountains. A late spring and early summer bloomer. FACTS/USES: The specific name, *uniflora*, means one-flowered. The root has known medicinal values, including use in a poultice for dog-bite wounds, and a tea also can be made to help expectant mothers during childbirth.

WARTBERRY FAIRY-BELL *Disporum trachycarpum*

This is an unusual perennial herb. The one- to two-foot stems ascend from thick underground rhizomes. The stems branch angularly into horizontal positions, and the end of each branch bears one or two small, white or cream-colored, bell-shaped flowers. The pendulous, six-tepaled flowers are inconspicuously hidden below the leaves on slender stems. Long, ovate or oblong, prominently veined leaves branch from the stem. A round, velvety berry containing six to 15 seeds develops from the flower. The berries are yellow at first, then turn red. HABITAT/RANGE: Fairy-bells often grow along stream banks or slopes of moist, shaded woods. Found from British Columbia to Alberta, the Dakotas, south to Colorado, New Mexico and Arizona. Blooms from late spring into early summer. FACTS/USES: The generic name is derived from the Greek word, *dis*, meaning double, and *spora*, for seed, referring to the two seeds per ovary cell.

GLACIER LILY   *Erythronium grandiflorum*

Glacier lilies are colorful and showy wildflowers. Six bright yellow tepals form a nodding flower at the end of a six- to 15-inch stalk. The tepals curl back and display six yellowish to purplish anthers. There usually are two basal leaves, which are shiny, long and broadly lanceolate. HABITAT/RANGE: This lily inhabits a wide variety of environments, from sagebrush to montane forests to subalpine meadows. It is a Western species, existing from British Columbia to Montana, south to Colorado and Oregon. Flowers from April to August, depending upon elevation. FACTS/USES: The Greek generic name is derived from *erythro*, meaning red, in reference to the pink or reddish color of some species. The starchy, elongated corms are a favorite food source, especially for grizzly bears, which rake their long claws through a patch to collect the bulbs. Indians used to cook or dry the corms for later consumption.

LEOPARD LILY   *Fritillaria atropurpurea*

Leopard lily is an unusual camouflaged flower. One to four brown, pendulous, bell-shaped flowers with purple, greenish and yellow mottled tepals help hide this flower. The one- to three-foot, erect stems have several very narrow, long, linear leaves. Stems ascend from bulb-like corms, usually surrounded by smaller bulblets. HABITAT/RANGE: Found on grassy slopes, coniferous forests and montane ridges to near timberline, it is distributed, but locally rare, from Washington to the Dakotas, south to Wyoming, New Mexico and central California. Flowers from late spring until early summer. FACTS/USES: The generic name, *Fritillaria*, is Latin for dice box, for its resemblance to the shape of the bell-like flowers. The specific name, *atropurpurea*, means dark purple. The corms of this species are surrounded by small seedlike bulblets. The starchy corms are edible but the plant is too rare to dig up.

YELLOW BELL   *Fritillaria pudica*

This small perennial arises three to eight inches from a starchy corm. The stem usually is unbranched and terminates in a pendulous or nodding bell-shaped flower. The six bright yellow tepals fade to reddish or purplish at maturity. The leaves are long, linear and thickened and usually are basal or midway along the stem. HABITAT/RANGE: An inhabitant of grassland, sagebrush plains, dry hillsides and coniferous forests. Distributed from British Columbia to Alberta, the Dakotas, Wyoming, Utah and northern California. One of the earliest spring bloomers, the yellow bell follows the snowline and usually is found with springbeauty *(Claytonia lanceolata)*. FACTS/USES: The specific name means bashful or retiring. The starchy bulbs or corms are edible and were known by Native Americans. The corms also are a favorite food for grizzly bears and pocket gophers.

RED LILY   *Lilium philadelphicum*
Red lily is one of the most colorful and rare species of the Rocky Mountains. The one- to two-foot, unbranched stems arise from fleshy-scaled bulbs. Long, narrow, lanceolate leaves are arranged alternately on the lower portion of the plant and in whorls near the top. Usually one, or sometimes several, large, orange-red, funnel-shaped blossoms with purple spots and large anthers terminate on the stem. HABITAT/RANGE: Occurs on moist grassland prairies, woods to mountain meadows. It is a rare plant, mainly because it has been reduced by grazing and picking. It now is found only locally along the eastern slopes of the Rocky Mountains, from Alberta to New Mexico, east to Saskatchewan, Ohio and Arkansas. Blooms from June to August. FACTS/USES: This plant may be in danger of extinction and should not be picked or transplanted because it usually does not survive transplanting.

WESTERN SOLOMON-PLUME   *Smilacina racemosa*
This species is very similar to *S. stellata*. The main difference is in the inflorescence and leaves. Numerous, tiny flowers are arranged in a dense panicle with each cream-colored flower having six minute tepals that are smaller than the filaments, or stalk, of the six stamens. Small quarter-inch, round, juicy, red-spotted berries develop from the flowers. The leaves are long, ovate, and clasp the stem. HABITAT/RANGE: This species prefers moist woods, stream banks and open forests from sea level to mid-mountain elevations. It is distributed from Alaska to Nova Scotia, south to Georgia, Missouri, Colorado and southern California. Flowers from April to July. FACTS/USES: The specific name, *racemosa*, means flowers in racemes. The young shoots, berries and roots are edible, if prepared properly.

STARRY SOLOMON-PLUME   *Smilacina stellata*
This plant has simple, terminal racemes with three to 15 small, whitish or cream-colored flowers arranged alternately along the peduncles. Each flower is comprised of three sepals and three petals that look alike; collectively, they are called tepals. A globose, greenish to red berry develops from the flower. The long, lance-shaped leaves are alternately arranged on a slender, unbranched, erect stem. The plants are rhizomatous perennial herbs. HABITAT/RANGE: An inhabitant of shaded, moist woods and stream banks to exposed hillsides of valleys and mountains. Found in cooler, moist climates throughout North America. Flowers from late spring to midsummer. FACTS/USES: The specific name means stellate or starry. The berries and roots are edible. Berries are best eaten cooked to reduce laxative effect, and Native Americans used to cook the bitter roots.

TWISTED-STALK   *Streptopus amplexifolius*
This is an unusual perennial wildflower of deep, shaded woods. The plant is characterized by a slender, zigzagging stem. At each bend of the stem branches a clasping, broad, ovate leaf with distinct parallel veins. Beneath the leaf axils are white, six-tepaled flowers on slender stalks that have a distinct twist or kink—hence the name twisted-stalk. The flower matures into a bright red berry. HABITAT/RANGE: It is a dweller of shady mountain thickets, most forests and the edges of stream banks. Twisted-stalk is distributed widely in North America, from Alaska to California. Flowers from late spring into midsummer. FACTS/USES: The Greek generic name is derived from *streptos*, meaning twisted, and *pous*, for foot, and refers to the bent flower stalks or peduncles; the specific name means leaf-clasping. The berries are browsed by grouse and other birds.

TRILLIUM   *Trillium ovatum*
Easily recognizable by its habitat and three broad, ovate leaves just below a white, three-petaled flower, the plant arises from short, thick rhizomes and reaches four to 15 inches high. The stems are erect, unbranched and terminate with a single white flower, which turns pinkish or red with age. The three leaves below the flower are whorled and stalkless. HABITAT/RANGE: This plant prefers moist, thick montane woods, especially along stream banks and boggy areas. Mostly found in the Central Rocky Mountains, from British Columbia to southern Alberta, south to Colorado and central California. A very early spring to early summer bloomer. FACTS/USES: The Latin generic name is derived from *tres*, meaning three. The specific name means ovate. The root of this plant is known for its medicinal qualities, such as a treatment for cramps or to reduce a swollen eye.

FALSE HELLEBORE   *Veratrum viride*
False hellebore is a large, cornstalk-like perennial herb that grows in dense patches and reaches three to six feet high. The conspicuous, large, broad leaves have deep, parallel veins that give the appearance of pleats. The small, six-tepaled, white or greenish flowers are densely clustered on a branched panicle. HABITAT/RANGE: False hellebore is found in wet thickets to swamps and lowlands to mountain meadows, and it ranges from Alaska to Maine, south to North Carolina, Colorado and Oregon. A similar and related species, *V. californicum*, is found in the southern range of the Rockies. Blooms from April to early August. FACTS/USES: This plant is extremely poisonous. Alkaloids concentrated in the root and young shoots often poison livestock in the early spring, when the plant is just emerging. False hellebore has been used medicinally as a heart depressant and spinal paralyzant. The chief reactant is veratrum, an alkaloid chemical.

BEARGRASS *Xerophyllum tenax*

This plant supports a dense, conical raceme of small, white or cream-colored flowers. A stout two- to four-foot stem ascends from a large basal tussock of grasslike leaves that are one to two feet long, strong and sharp-edged. The erect stems often persist through the next season. HABITAT/RANGE: This mountain plant grows best on well-drained slopes and ridges. It ranges from British Columbia, Montana and Nevada to central California. Beargrass begins to bloom at lower elevations, about 3,000 feet, in June and continues into August at elevations of 8,000 feet. FACTS/USES: The name beargrass refers to bears digging the starchy rhizomes in spring and to the grasslike leaves. The generic name, *Xerophyllum*, refers to the leaves being dry and tough. Native Americans used this plant by roasting the roots for food and by drying and bleaching the leaves for weaving and padding.

MEADOW DEATH-CAMAS *Zigadenus venenosus*

This plant is a perennial herb with a dense raceme of small whitish or cream-colored flowers. The six- to 20-inch, unbranched, erect stems arise from small, onion-like bulbs. The leaves are narrow, linear, grasslike blades that grow from the base with smaller leaves along the stem. HABITAT/RANGE: Death camas has a wide variation of habitats—from plains, grassy foothills, sagebrush slopes to montane forests and alpine meadows. It is distributed widely throughout the West, from British Columbia to Saskatchewan, south to Nebraska, Colorado and Baja, California. Flowers from early spring to midsummer. FACTS/USES: The specific name means poisonous. Next to hemlock, this is the most poisonous plant in the West. The active agent is an alkaloid called zygadenine, which causes a quickening and irregularity of the heartbeat, slow respiration and convulsions.

Iris Family
Iridaceae

ROCKY MOUNTAIN IRIS *Iris missouriensis*

Rocky Mountain iris is a large and stately perennial herb with dark, thickened, fibrous rhizomes and long, equitant, sword-shaped leaves. The eight- to 24-inch fleshy, leafless stalk is topped with a large, attractive blue flower with dark blue veins, plus three petallike sepals curving downward and three smaller, erect petals. HABITAT/RANGE: This species inhabits moist meadows and stream banks that have a tendency to dry by midsummer and is found in small, isolated patches from the eastern slopes of the Cascade Range to the Dakotas and south to New Mexico and southern California. An early spring bloomer beginning in mid-May in lower elevations to mid-July in higher elevations. FACTS/USES: Other closely related species of European iris have been used as ornamental hybrids and for medicinal purposes. An extract from the rhizome is used as a potent cathartic and emetic.

BLUE-EYED GRASS   *Sisyrinchium angustifolium*

This species is a grasslike plant with small, blue, starlike flowers, seldom more than a half-inch across. Each flower is composed of three petals and three sepals, which look alike. The flattened stalks can reach four to 20 inches in height, with shorter, swordlike basal leaves. HABITAT/RANGE: Blue-eyed grass prefers marshes and ditches, where it is always moist in the spring and drying by midsummer. Found from southern Alaska across Canada and along the eastern slope of the Rocky Mountains to Baja, California. Blooms from May until July from sea level to montane meadows. FACTS/USES: The specific name, *angustifolium*, means narrow leaf. As a group, blue-eyed grass is extremely variable, ranging in color from white to deep purple and having growth irregularities due to extreme environmental conditions. Because of this variability, botanists often separate variants within an integrated species.

Orchid Family
Orchidaceae

FAIRY-SLIPPER   *Calypso bulbosa*

This showy, colorful wildflower of deep, dark woods has a pinkish-brown, sheathed stalk, two to four inches tall, arising from a small corm. The stalk supports a terminal slipper-shaped flower with rose and brown stripes. Another distinguishing characteristic is the single, broad, basal leaf that emerges when the plant flowers. HABITAT/RANGE: An inhabitant of cool, moist, deep shaded, north-facing slopes of forests, from sea level to montane zones. Though rare, it is a circumboreal flower found in North America, from Alaska to Labrador, south to New York, Minnesota, Colorado, New Mexico, Arizona and California. Blooms from mid-May through June. FACTS/USES: Calypso is named for the sea nymph, Kalypso, which means covered or hidden from view. The specific name, *bulbosa*, means bulbous, referring to the bulb-like corm. The plant is rare and should not be picked but the corms are edible.

SPOTTED CORAL-ROOT   *Corallorhiza maculata*

Several erect six- to 24-inch stalks grow in clumps among decaying duff of deep woods. The reddish wine-colored stalks are leafless—except for membranous bracts at the base of the stalk—and bear small orchids along an open raceme. This species is very similar to Western coral-root, but the lower lip of this flower is white with purple spots. HABITAT/RANGE: This plant is a saprophyte, living on dead or decaying organic matter, thus its habitat is moist to dry woods with humus and duff layers. It is spread widely from British Columbia to Nova Scotia, south to North Carolina, Indiana, New Mexico, and southern California. It also is found in Central America. Flowers from late May to late July. FACTS/USES: The specific name means spotted. Coral-root refers to the coral-like rhizomes that associate with fungus and help in the decay of organic matter, thus allowing absorption of nutrients.

WESTERN CORAL-ROOT   *Corallorhiza mertensiana*

This perennial forb ascends six to 24 inches from extensive coral-like rhizomes. The erect, reddish stalks lack chlorophyll and leaves, except for several membranous bracts on the lower stalk. Small, reddish orchids are arranged sparingly in a raceme. Each small flower is comprised of a funnel—formed by sepals and petals fused together—with a small spur projecting underneath. Two lateral lobes spread outward, while a cap projects downward from the top and a reddish- and white-lobed lip flares down. HABITAT/RANGE: Mostly found in moist coniferous forests, often standing in a spot of sunlight. It also requires decaying humus or duff for nutrients. Widely distributed in the West, from Alaska to Montana, Wyoming and California. An early to midsummer bloomer. FACTS/USES: The generic name, *Corallorhiza*, is derived from the Greek, *korallion*, meaning coral, and *rhiza*, for root.

STRIPED CORAL-ROOT   *Corallorhiza striata*

Striped coral-root is an unusual orchid. It is a leafless plant that bears small membranous bracts along the erect, pinkish stalks and a sparse raceme of small orchids. Each flower has reddish-brown, striped tepals, the lowest one broadening into a lip that is not lobed. A spur also is lacking in this species. HABITAT/RANGE: It is a dweller of deep, shaded coniferous and deciduous woods with rich humus and duff layers. Striped coral-root is well-distributed from British Columbia across southern Canada to Quebec, south to Michigan, Colorado, New Mexico and California. Blooms from late May to mid-August. FACTS/USES: The specific name, *striata*, means striated or striped. The plants are without leaves and chlorophyll; they lack green color but absorb nutrients through their roots with the aid of a fungus that also helps in the decaying process.

WHITE BOG-ORCHID   *Habenaria dilata*

This bright white orchid of boggy and wet seeps has an unbranched stem arising one to two feet from short tuberous roots. The tall, narrow plant features a dense, slender spike of white orchid flowers, which contrast with the bright green foliage. Each waxy, white flower is hooded by lateral lobes and a lip with a prominent spur projecting underneath. Long, narrow leaves clasp the stem. HABITAT/RANGE: Several stems of white bog-orchids often are found growing together in very lush, wet, boggy springs or seeps. They are distributed widely from Alaska to Greenland, south to New York, Michigan, South Dakota, New Mexico and California. Flower through the summer. FACTS/USES: The Latin generic name is derived from *habena*, which means reins or narrow straps and refers to the narrow lip of some of the species. The specific name means dilated or expanded, referring to the flaring lobes.

LADIES-TRESSES   *Spiranthes romanzoffiana*
This distinctive and unusual orchid of bogs and swamps features small, whitish, orchid flowers arranged in a dense spike that spirals, or twists, in longitudinal rows like a barber pole. The flowers are in the shape of a funnel, with a hood and a small lip. The stems usually are four to 18 inches tall with bright green, narrow, lance-shaped, basal or cauline leaves. HABITAT/RANGE: Ladies-tresses ranges from wet, boggy seeps along streams to grassy meadows and, in elevation, from coastal salt flats to high mountain meadows. It is distributed from Alaska to Newfoundland, south to New York, Wisconsin, Montana, Arizona and California. Blooms from mid to late summer. FACTS/USES: The specific name is derived from the Greek word, *speira*, meaning coil, and *anthos*, for flower, referring to the spiral inflorescence. It is believed that the spiral formation is the result of uneven cell growth.

Mistletoe Family
Loranthaceae

AMERICAN DWARF MISTLETOE *Arceuthobium americanum*
This is an unusual and easily missed flower. A parasite on the limbs of conifers, the plant is small—a quarter-inch to one foot high, fleshy, and yellowish-brown. The stems are four-angled and swollen-jointed with opposite, scalelike leaves. The dioecious plants—male and female flowers borne on separate plants—have tiny, yellow flowers arranged in the axils of the scales. The fruit is a small, fleshy, bluish, ovoid berry. When the berry matures, it explodes, ejecting a single seed that has a sticky pulp and becomes attached to another limb or another tree. HABITAT/RANGE: This species prefers one particular host, lodgepole pine *(Pinus contorta)*, and follows its range. Other species of mistletoe also have adapted to specific hosts. Blooms early spring to midsummer. FACTS/USES: After many years of growth, dwarf mistletoe forms dense, tangled clusters, called "witches broom."

Buckwheat Family
Polygonaceae

SULFUR BUCKWHEAT   *Eriogonum umbellatum*
Sulfur buckwheat forms dense, low mats of small, half- to one-inch, lanceolate or spatulate leaves. Each leaf is green on the top and densely woolly on the bottom, giving it a silver-gray appearance. From the perennial roots and the creeping woody branches that form the leafy mat ascend one or more erect, leafless, woolly stems. Each stem terminates in a whorl of bract-like leaves, which branch into an umbel. Each peduncle then bears a ball-like cluster of tiny yellow flowers. HABITAT/RANGE: This plant has a wide variety of habitats, from sagebrush plains to rocky alpine ridges. It is found from southern British Columbia to Montana, south to Colorado, Arizona and California. Flowers from late May to August. FACTS/USES: The generic name is derived from the Greek word, *erion*, meaning wool, and *gonu*, for knee, referring to the woolly nodes and stems of many species.

MOUNTAIN SORREL   *Oxyria digyna*
Mountain sorrel is a perennial herb with mostly basal leaves. The roundish or kidney-shaped leaves are glabrous, often reddish-tinged and on long, fleshy leafstalks. The plants are four to 12 inches tall, and the stems bear a dense panicled raceme of small red or greenish flowers. The flowers develop into a conspicuous fruit—a flat achene with broad, membranous wings that turn a bright red-rose color on maturity. HABITAT/RANGE: A dweller of gravelly or stony, moist, cold subalpine and alpine regions. Mountain sorrel is a circumboreal species found from Alaska across Canada to Labrador, south to New Hampshire, Michigan and New Mexico. Flowers during midsummer. FACTS/USES: The generic name is derived from the Greek word, *oxys*, meaning sharp and referring to the acidic juice of this plant. The leaves are edible and have a pleasant sour taste when eaten raw in salads. They also are high in vitamin C.

WATER SMARTWEED   *Polygonum amphibium*
Water smartweed is an aquatic or semiaquatic plant with floating, oval leaves and may grow semi-submerged in shallow water or, more commonly, on mud flats. A long prostrate or erect stem—up to seven feet long—bears a terminal spike of bright pink flowers. HABITAT/RANGE: Water smartweed is a cosmopolitan species found on muddy banks and shallow ponds, from plains to montane environments. It occurs from Alaska to Quebec, south to Pennsylvania, New Mexico and California. Blooms from late June to mid-September. FACTS/USES: The generic name, *Polygonum*, is derived from the Greek words, *polus*, meaning many, and *gonu*, meaning knee. This refers to the swollen joints, or nodes, characteristic of this genera. Roots often sprout from the joints to anchor the plant to mud flats. Water smartweed grows quickly and, by late summer, a dense mat of aquatic vegetation can cover a shallow pond. The seeds are important food for ducks.

AMERICAN BISTORT   *Polygonum bistortoides*
American bistort is a slender perennial plant with a snakelike, thick rhizome. Most of the narrow, tapering leaves are basal and a few follow the narrow stem to a densely clustered raceme of small white to pinkish flowers. The racemes often rise above the subalpine turf and sway in the wind. HABITAT/RANGE: A common dweller of the mountains, especially of shady woods, stream banks and alpine meadows. It is distributed from British Columbia to Alberta, south to New Mexico and California. Blooms from June to August. FACTS/USES: The specific name, *bistortoides*, means twice twisted, referring to the twisted appearance of the small flowers along the raceme. A circumboreal European species, *P. viviparum*, is closely related and similar in appearance. The starchy rhizomes are edible raw, boiled or roasted, and the young leaves and shoots can be used as greens or a potherb.

CURLY DOCK   *Rumex crispus*

Curly dock is a stout, leafy, erect perennial herb with a dense panicled raceme; the small greenish flowers are borne on long, slender pedicels clustered in whorls. A flower matures to a conspicuous reddish-brown fruit, which is an achene surrounded by three heart-shaped, winglike appendages. The dark green leaves have a characteristic curly or crisp margin. The reddish stems ascend one to three feet from a large, yellow, somewhat branched taproot. HABITAT/RANGE: This widespread plant— introduced and naturalized from Eurasia—is well-adapted to establishing on disturbed sites in pastures, meadows, and along trails and roads, from lowland areas into the lower mountains. Blooms from June to September. FACTS/USES: *Rumex* is an ancient Latin name for this group. The specific name means crisped or curled. The leaves are edible and make an excellent potherb.

Purslane Family
Portulaceaceae

SPRINGBEAUTY   *Claytonia lanceolata*

This conspicuous pink to white flower is a delicate perennial herb that stands three to seven inches tall. The long, narrow, lanceolate leaves are opposite at mid-stem. The loose raceme bears three to 15 buds or flowers on long pedicles. The root is a starchy, fleshy corm about half an inch to one inch in diameter. HABITAT/RANGE: Springbeauty is one of the first flowers to appear in the spring and follows the snowline up the mountains, blooming into late July in alpine meadows. It is very common and widely distributed from British Columbia to Alberta, south to New Mexico and California. FACTS/USES: Western pioneers called it Indian potato because the tubers reminded them of the European potato. When eaten raw, the corms are crisp like potatoes, but sweet. When boiled in water for 25 minutes, they taste even better. Wildlife including the marmot, grizzly bear, and ground squirrels enjoy it as well.

ALPINE LEWISIA   *Lewisia pygmaea*

Alpine Lewisia is a very low plant with one or several flower stems nestled among the narrow, fleshy, basal leaves. Each stem has a pair of opposite bracts partway up and graces a single blossom that usually possesses seven bright pink—but occasionally white, greenish-white or lavender—petals. The fleshy leaves usually remain green during the blooming cycle. HABITAT/RANGE: It generally is found on gravelly slopes of moist to dry ridges in subalpine and alpine habitats. Distributed in the southern Canadian Rockies to New Mexico and southern California. Blooms between late May and mid-August. FACTS/USES: This flower looks very similar to springbeauty *(Claytonia lanceolata)*, but alpine Lewisia generally has seven petals and a two-cleft style. *Pygmaea* means dwarf.

BITTERROOT   *Lewisia rediviva*

This low-growing, succulent, perennial herb bears a cluster of large, showy, 12- to 16-petalled, rose- or pink-colored blossoms. The numerous basal leaves are smooth, succulent and nearly round when they first appear in early spring. The leaves then dry up, recede, and vanish as the flowers appear by May. It has a large, thick, branching taproot. HABITAT/RANGE: Bitterroot prefers prairies, gravelly benches and river bars at lower elevations, and stony slopes and open windswept ridges at lower mountain elevations. It is locally abundant and found from British Columbia to eastern Montana, south to Arizona and California. FACTS/USES: This plant was named in honor of Capt. Meriwether Lewis, who first described it in 1806 during his northwest expedition. Bitterroot, aptly named, was an important economic plant for Native Americans. It is the state flower of Montana.

Pink Family
Carophyllaceae

BALLHEAD SANDWORT   *Arenaria congesta*

This species arises from a tuft of long, narrow, sharp-pointed, grasslike leaves with two to four pairs of smaller, opposite leaves along the stem. The erect, slender, six- to 20-inch stem terminates in a congested inflorescence of white flowers. Each small flower consists of five sepals that are half the length of the five petals, and 10 stamens. HABITAT/RANGE: It has a wide range of habitats, from sagebrush desert to alpine slopes, but prefers sandy, moderately dry soils and often is found among sedges and grasses of lodgepole or ponderosa pines. It is distributed from Washington to Montana, south to Colorado and Utah. Flowers throughout the summer. FACTS/USES: The generic name is derived from the Latin word, *arena*, meaning sand, and refers to the sandy soils this plant prefers. The specific name, *congesta*, means congested or brought together, in reference to the flower heads.

NUTTALL'S SANDWORT   *Arenaria nuttallii*

Nuttall's sandwort is a small, tufted, mat-forming perennial herb. The stems are somewhat woody at the base and trail along the ground before ascending, seldom more than five inches high, as a flowering stalk. The white flowers often are congested near the top but do not bloom simultaneously. Each flower is comprised of five lanceolate, sharp-pointed sepals and are the same length as the five petals. The small leaves are pungent and linear or lanceolate in shape. HABITAT/RANGE: This plant prefers gravelly soils of benches or talus, from sagebrush slopes to alpine ridges. It is distributed from British Columbia to Alberta, south to Utah and Nevada. Flowers throughout the summer, depending upon the elevation. FACTS/USES: Species of the sandwort group are difficult to differentiate but generally are identified by their narrow, opposite leaves, five petals, 10 stamens and a three-styled ovary.

FIELD CHICKWEED   *Cerastium arvense*

Field chickweed is a lax, spindly perennial herb, often growing in clustered, somewhat matted patches. At the end of the three- to 15-inch stem generally are one to several white flowers. Each flower, nearly an inch long, has five sepals, half the length of the five petals. The petals have a distinguishing deep notch at the tip. The leaves are opposite, narrow and lanceolate in shape and often glandular with short hairs. The fruit is a one-celled capsule. HABITAT/RANGE: It is found from sandy-salty coastal cliffs to gravelly subalpine slopes. This is a circumboreal species distributed through Canada and south to New Mexico and northern California. Blooms from spring to late summer. FACTS/USES: The generic name, *Cerastium*, is derived from the Greek word, *keras*, which means horn, and refers to the slender curved capsuled fruit. *Arvense* means pertaining to cultivated fields.

WHITE CAMPION   *Lychnis alba*

White campion is a biennial or a short-lived perennial herb that reproduces by seed. The one- to three-foot stems bear opposite, lanceolate leaves, with the plant covered in glandular hairs. The branching flower stems are arranged in a cyme with white or pinkish flowers. The flowers have a long, striped, glandular-hairy calyx tube and five petals deeply notched at the tip. The male and female flowering parts are borne on separate plants. HABITAT/RANGE: This introduced and naturalized plant from Eurasia establishes well along roads and other disturbed sites. It is distributed throughout the northern half of the United States and southern Canada. In the West, it is found as far south as Colorado and central California and is extending its range. FACTS/USES: The generic name, *Lychnis*, is derived from the Greek word, *lychnos*, for lamp, in reference to the bright flowers.

MOSS CAMPION   *Silene acaulis*

This small plant forms a mossy, firm cushion of many narrow, opposite, acute leaves. The roots and trailing stems are woody, and the plant does not exceed three or four inches in height. Each flowering stem terminates in a single pinkish flower, and the numerous flowers often cover the entire cushion plant. The flowers are comprised of five petals and 10 light yellow stamens. This plant easily can be confused with Rocky Mountain douglasia *(Douglasia montana)*, which has five stamens opposite the petals. HABITAT/RANGE: This is a circumpolar, alpine-arctic species that prefers rock crevices or talus above timberline. It is a cordilleran species found throughout Canada and as far south as New Hampshire, New Mexico and Oregon. Blooms through the summer, depending upon elevation. FACTS/USES: The specific name, *acaulis*, means stemless, referring to its short, mat-forming growth.

Waterlily Family
Nymphaeceae

YELLOW POND LILY   *Nuphar polysepalum*

Yellow pond lily is easily recognized by its baseball-sized yellow flower and large, leathery, heart-shaped leaves. Although it appears to float on the surface of a pond, it actually is attached by long, fleshy rootstocks buried in the mud four to five feet below the water's surface. HABITAT/RANGE: Common in beaver ponds and other slow-moving water courses from lowlands into the mountains and from Alaska to Colorado. Blooms from mid-June into August. FACTS/USES: When the flowers mature into seed-bearing pods, Native Americans then harvested the pods from a canoe. After the pods dried, the seeds could be removed easily. They then were fried over a slow fire, and allowed to pop, much like our popcorn in taste and appearance. Indians also were known to grind the root into meal or flour. Muskrats gather rootstocks and store them in their lodges for winter.

Buttercup Family
Ranunculaceae

MONKSHOOD   *Aconitum columbianum*

The white to purple, hoodlike flowers make this an unusual and easily recognizable plant. The flowers are arranged in loose racemes on tall, stout stems, two to five feet tall. The five sepals, resembling petals—the petals actually are hidden within the flower or they are mere vestiges—are colorful, and the upper sepal forms a monk's hood, as worn by medieval monks. The leaves are large, two to eight inches wide, and palmately three- to five-lobed with lance-shaped teeth. HABITAT/RANGE: Monkshood is a dweller of moist woods and stream banks to subalpine meadows. Widely distributed from Alaska to Alberta, south to New Mexico and California, it blooms from early June until late July. FACTS/USES: This plant is considered poisonous to wildlife but it seldom is consumed in enough quantity to cause serious harm. The poisonous toxin is aconite.

BANEBERRY   *Actaea rubra*

This erect, leafy, perennial herb arises one to three feet from a thick, branching rootstock. The large leaves are pinnately divided, mostly into threes, with each leaflet sharply toothed. Tiny whitish or cream-colored flowers are arranged in a terminal raceme. The petallike sepals (petals are smaller and inconspicuous) are short-lived and drop off soon after flowering. The ovary matures to a berry that contains several large seeds. When ripe, the berries vary in color from white to red—or the two colors swirled together. HABITAT/RANGE: Baneberry prefers moist sites along streams, especially in shaded woods. It is distributed widely from Alaska across Canada and the northern United States, south to New Mexico and California. Blooms from May to July. FACTS/USES: The specific name means sharp-toothed. The moderately poisonous berries can cause cardiac arrest.

CLIFF ANEMONE
Anemone multifida

Cliff anemone is a herbaceous perennial ascending from thick, woody taproots year after year. The five to nine sepals are colorful, ranging from cream to deep rose-pink or red to purple. One to three flowers usually are borne at the end of an eight- to 20-inch silky-hairy stem. The leaves generally are basal on long peticles or they form a dense involucre on the flowering stem. Each leaf is divided into three or more long, linear, lanceolate lobes. The seed heads are conspicuous globe-shaped cotton balls, composed of acenes that form dense white-woolly cotton. HABITAT/RANGE: Found on a wide range of habitats from foothills to alpine, it prefers dry to moist soils and sunny sites. It can be abundant locally when it flowers during midsummer and is well-distributed from Alaska across southern Canada and south to New Mexico, California and even into South America. FACTS/USES: The specific name means parted many times.

PASQUEFLOWER
Anemone nuttalliana

Pasqueflower is a short—up to one foot tall—and hairy plant with several stout, thick stems growing from perennial taproots. The leaves are mainly basal, with three leaves in a whorl just below the flower. Each silky leaf is deeply dissected into narrow fingerlike lobes. Each stem terminates in a cup-shaped, silky, lavender-blue flower with numerous yellow stamens. As the flower matures, the sepals turn brown and a long, plumose, feather-like fruit develops. HABITAT/RANGE: One of the earliest spring bloomers, it pushes through old, weathered grass in well-drained soils of prairies or mountain meadows. Found from Washington to Alaska, along the northern plains to Illinois, and the eastern slope of the Rocky Mountains to Texas. FACTS/USES: Pasqueflower is derived from the old form of the word *pasch* and refers to the feast of the Passover at Easter. Native Americans had many medicinal uses for this plant.

COLORADO COLUMBINE
Aquilegia coerulea

Colorado columbine is a perennial herb with a bushy appearance and showy flowers. The five white to blue sepals flare outward, with five whitish to cream-colored petals that form long one- to two-inch spurs projecting backward between the sepals. The plants grow two to three feet tall and have mostly long, peticled basal leaves that are divided into deeply cleft, round-lobed leaflets. HABITAT/RANGE: It grows in moist meadows, open woods, along streams or among rocky crevices. Mainly a Rocky Mountain species, it is found in Idaho and western Montana, south to Colorado and New Mexico. Flowers June to August. FACTS/USES: Colorado columbine is the state flower of Colorado. Native Americans, especially bachelors, used the seeds as a perfume. They obtained the odor by crushing or chewing the seeds into a paste. The paste then was spread among clothes, where the fragrance would linger.

YELLOW COLUMBINE   *Aquilegia flavescens*
This flower is similar in appearance to Colorado columbine, except the sepals are reddish and the hollow spurs of the petals are yellow. The fruit is a hairy pod, containing many seeds. HABITAT/RANGE: This common wildflower prefers moist, acidic soils of rocky ledges and screes, mountain meadows and alpine slopes. It is distributed from British Columbia to Alberta, south to Colorado, Utah and Eastern Oregon. Blooms from June to August. FACTS/USES: The generic name is derived from the Latin word, *aquila*, meaning eagle, and refers to the eagle-like spurs or claws of the flower. Columbine has a number of medicinal uses. Tea made from the roots and leaves is good for diarrhea, or most any kind of stomach and bowel troubles. To cure a headache, a tea can be brewed by gathering the tiny black seeds and crushing them in hot water. The dried roots can be used to cause perspiration on the skin.

MARSHMARIGOLD   *Caltha Leptosepala*
The white buttercup-like flowers arise from a basal cluster of heart-shaped, green, fleshy leaves on a pinkish, naked stalk one to eight inches high. The flowers are one to two inches wide and lack petals, but the five to 12 sepals are showy white. HABITAT/RANGE: A common wildflower growing in dense mats along stream banks in wet alpine and subalpine meadows; it's found from Alaska to Alberta and south to New Mexico, Arizona and Oregon. Flowers from late May until early August, depending upon latitude. FACTS/USES: The generic name, *caltha*, is from an early Greek name for a yellow-flowered species, and the specific name means thin-sepaled. The eastern species of marshmarigold *(C. palustris)* was cooked and eaten by Native Americans and early settlers. Our Western species is, however, more bitter and possibly toxic, due to poisonous glucosides, and so is not widely known as a food plant for people.

COLUMBIA CLEMATIS *Clematis columbiana (occidentalis)*
This perennial, woody, creeping vine may grow to 10 feet in length. The large, two-inch-diameter, pale purple flowers are borne singly on a peduncle that stems from leaf axils. Each flower is comprised of four showy, long, lanceolate sepals (there are no petals), which flare outward to reveal a cluster of numerous yellow stamens. The ovary styles elongate into a feathery plume. The opposite leaves are compound, with three broad lanceolate leaflets. HABITAT/RANGE: Clematis is a climbing vine and usually drapes over stumps and fallen trees. It prefers dry to moist soils of shrubby or wooded sites of foothills to the montane zone. It's a common flower from British Columbia to Montana and south to Colorado, Utah and Oregon. Blooms May to July. FACTS/USES: The specific name, *columbiana*, refers to the Columbia River drainage or the region west of the Continental Divide. *Occidentalis* means western.

SUGARBOWLS   *Clematis hirsutissima*
Sugarbowls are a low, bush-like, herbaceous perennial. The one- to two-foot-tall leafy stems terminate with a single, nodding, leathery flower. Each flower is two-toned. The outside of the four sepals have a grayish pubescence (this genera lacks petals), while the inside is dark purple or maroon. The sepals flare outward and give the flower a "sugarbowl" appearance. The leaves are finely dissected into fingerlike projections with a silver, hairy covering. The styles elongate into feathery plumes nearly two inches long, with each plume bearing a single achene. HABITAT/RANGE: It is found on dry grasslands and sagebrush deserts to montane forests. Distributed from Oregon and British Columbia to Montana, south to northern New Mexico and Arizona. A spring and early summer bloomer. FACTS/USES: The specific name, *hirsutissima*, means very hairy.

VIRGIN'S BOWER   *Clematis ligusticifolia*
Virgin's bower is a clambering woody vine that grows to a length of 10 to 20 feet. At times, the plant can cover or engulf its support shrub, tree, or fence and, when in full bloom, is covered with a profusion of cream-colored flowers. The flowers have four or five showy sepals, with no petals, and staminate and pistillate flowers on separate plants. As the flower matures, the style of the pistil elongates into a tan one- to two-inch plume. The leaves are opposite and pinnately compound into five to seven toothed leaflets. HABITAT/RANGE: This species is found along creek bottoms, sagebrush deserts to ponderosa pine forests. It is well-distributed from British Columbia to the Dakotas, south to New Mexico and California. Flowers May to August. FACTS/USES: This plant was used medicinally by Native Americans for sore throats, colds, and as a tonic brew.

LITTLE LARKSPUR   *Delphinium bicolor*
This flower is very similar to upland larkspur *(D. nuttallianum)*. The main difference is that the two small lower petals, which overlap the two large lower sepals, are deep blue and have a shallow notch. The sepals, too, are unequal, the lower pair being the longest. HABITAT/RANGE: A dweller of grasslands and ponderosa pine forests to subalpine meadows and scree. It has a small range, from Alberta to Saskatchewan, South Dakota to Wyoming and central Idaho. Flowers in May and June. FACTS/USES: There is an old Greek legend behind the genus name: The Greeks believed that a fisherman lost his life while saving a dolphin from being captured. In return, the dolphin carried the man's body on its back to the god, Neptune, and begged that he be restored to life in some manner. Neptune thus turned him into a flower that is the color of the sea and whose bud is shaped like a dolphin with a load on its back.

UPLAND LARKSPUR   *Delphinium nuttallianum*

Upland larkspur is a rather showy flower with large dark blue or purplish, irregular flowers and an upper sepal projecting backward as a spur. The common name refers to this prolonged sepal, comparing it to the spur on the foot of a lark. The stems are seven to 16 inches tall, with finely hairy, fingerlike lobed leaves that originate from the base or along the stem. HABITAT/RANGE: Its habitat is varied from dry to moist sagebrush deserts to mountain valleys and slopes. It is found from British Columbia to Alberta, south to Wyoming, Nebraska, Arizona and California. Blooms from early spring to early summer. FACTS/USES: All parts of this plant contain poisonous alkaloids, mainly delphinine, and it is considered highly toxic to cattle in the spring, but not poisonous to domestic sheep. Early settlers used the seeds as poison baits in exterminating lice.

DUNCECAP LARKSPUR   *Delphinium occidentale*

Duncecap larkspur is a very tall, stout perennial herb that reaches a height of three to six feet. The whitish-streaked or pale-blue flowers have five petallike sepals, with the upper sepal projecting backward into a hollow spur. The leaves are palmately divided into five to seven lobes, which usually are lance or diamond-shaped and finely hairy. HABITAT/RANGE: This plant prefers rich loam soils of moist mountain meadows or stream banks and flourishes in open or shaded sites. It often is associated with aspen stands. Distributed throughout the western United States, except for the southern states. Blooms during June and July. FACTS/USES: The Latin specific name means western, referring to the plant's range. This species is considered highly poisonous to livestock, especially when they graze mountain meadows in the early spring, as new shoots are emerging.

SUBALPINE BUTTERCUP   *Ranunculus eschscholtzii*

This perennial plant has brilliant, shiny yellow flowers that fade to white as they mature. The leaves help distinguish this species from the other numerous buttercups. The leaves are three-lobed; the middle lobe may be divided again into three segments or undivided; and the side lobes are divided into three to seven segments, making the leaves appear as numerous narrow fingers. HABITAT/RANGE: A plant of moist mountain meadows, ridges, and talus slopes. Varying in height from two to 12 inches due to environmental extremes, this widely dispersed mountain flower grows from Alaska to Alberta, south to New Mexico and southern California. Blooms late June to early August. FACTS/USES: Buttercups are considered poisonous, though the toxicity depends on the species and the part of the plant, with the flowers being the most toxic. The toxin, protoanemonin, dissipates when the plant is boiled or dried.

WATER BUTTERCUP   *Ranunculus aquatilis*
Easily identified by its aquatic habitat, this plant is mainly submersed, with the brownish stems and finely divided leaves floating on the surface of the water. The small, delicate, five-petaled, white flowers are held above the water by stalks. The plant grows in dense patches and can bear a profuse number of white blossoms that gently wave in the current. HABITAT/RANGE: A native of sluggish streams and ponds from lowlands to higher elevations throughout much of North America and Europe, it blooms from May until August, depending upon elevation. FACTS/USES: The genus *Ranunculus* was named by the first-century Roman scholar, Pliny. The Latin specific name is derived from *rana*, meaning frog, in reference to most of the species' aquatic habits. This plant provides excellent breeding beds for aquatic insects, which, in turn, provide food for trout and waterfowl.

SAGEBRUSH BUTTERCUP   *Ranunculus glaberrimus*
This shiny, bright yellow, five-petaled and many-stamened flower is one of the first plants to appear in the spring, following the receding snow. The long, fleshy basal leaves are elliptic to roundish in shape, and the stem leaves are three-lobed. The two- to eight-inch plant ascends from thick, fleshy roots and, in the fall, new shoots, or buds, form and remain dormant under the snow until spring. HABITAT/RANGE: This flower is one of the earliest spring bloomers of sagebrush and grasslands and blooms during summer in mountain meadows. It is distributed widely from British Columbia to the Dakotas, Nebraska, New Mexico and California. FACTS/USES: The specific name, *glabberimus*, means very smooth, referring to the waxy-shiny appearance of the flowers and leaves. The common name of buttercup comes from the resemblance of the shiny yellow flowers to a cup of butter.

WESTERN MEADOWRUE   *Thalictrum occidentale*
The greenish, whitish or purplish flowers, while lacking petals, are clustered in loose, terminal panicles. The male (stamen) and female (pistil) flowers are borne on separate plants (dioecious). The male flowers are very attractive, resembling old-fashioned lamp shades with tassels, while the female flowers resemble a Medusa head of snakes. There are seven species of meadowrues in the West and a few species are perfect, containing both female and male parts. The compound leaves are divided into roundish, three-lobed leaflets. HABITAT/RANGE: A dweller of moist, shaded woods and mountain streams. Common from British Columbia to Alberta, south to Utah and California, it blooms from May to July. FACTS/USES: Native bachelors rubbed the tops of meadowrue with saliva into their palms to capture the love and affection of a desired maiden by shaking hands with her.

GLOBEFLOWER
Trollius laxus

Globeflower is a perennial herb that grows in clumps with five to nine whitish or yellowish petallike sepals, which often become dingy when they begin to fade. The leaves are palmately cleft into five lobes, which again are deeply toothed. Both leaves and stems are glabrous with the clustered stems each bearing a single terminal flower. HABITAT/RANGE: This inhabitant of swamps and streams to above timberline in wet alpine meadows is distributed from Oregon, Washington, British Columbia and east to Connecticut and south along the Rocky Mountains to Colorado. Blossoms in the early spring near snowline. FACTS/USES: The specific name mans lax, open or loose, referring to the open flowers. The common globeflower, however, comes from other garden species, which have a round or globe-like shape. Globeflower easily can be confused with marshmarigold.

Barberry Family
Berberidaceae

CREEPING OREGONGRAPE
Berberis repens

This low, spreading shrub has glossy evergreen leaves that turn red or maroon during winter. The compound leaves have five to seven holly-like leaflets branching from a stem less than a foot tall. The stem has a yellowish inner bark. Clusters of bright, small yellow flowers branch from the stem and mature to glaucous blue berries. HABITAT/RANGE: Inhabits moderately dry soils of open pine forests from low foothills to montane forests. It is distributed widely in the West, from British Columbia to Alberta, South Dakota and south to Texas and California. Spring and early summer bloomer. FACTS/USES: The berries of this species have a sour grape-like flavor and, with plenty of sweetener, make good jelly. The yellow inner bark was used by Native Americans as a dye, while the roots were used for stomach troubles and as a blood purifier.

Bleeding Heart Family
Fumariaceae

STEER'S HEAD
Dicentra uniflora

Steer's head, a tiny plant only several inches tall, is over-looked easily. The stems arise from a rhizomatous, carrot-like root, with a single flower on each stem. Each white to purplish flower resembles an upside down steer's skull with horns, but there actually are four petals arranged in two pairs. The outer pair are narrow and curve outward (horns) and the inner pair are broad at the base, narrowing at the apex (skull). The basal leaves are finely dissected. HABITAT/RANGE: This plant associates with sagebrush and prefers well-drained soils of foothills to subalpine slopes. It is found from Washington to western Wyoming, south to Utah and northern California. An early spring bloomer, it follows the snowline. FACTS/USES: The generic name is derived form the Greek words *dis*, meaning twice, and *kentron*, meaning spur, referring to the spurs or outer petals.

Mustard Family
Brassicaceae

DRUMMOND'S ROCKCRESS   *Arabis drummondii*

A slender, biennial herb ascending from a branched taproot, the basal rosette is comprised of narrow spatulate leaves, while the stem leaves are somewhat larger and clasp the stem. Near the base of the plant are minute hairs, which are horizontal and attached at the middle. The small, white to pinkish flowers are clustered at the end of the stem, with the lower flowers maturing into fruit first. The siliques (pods) are erect in a compact cluster one to four inches long and one-eighth inch wide. HABITAT/RANGE: Rockcress inhabits moist to wet rocky slopes from montane to subalpine zones. It is found throughout the West, across southern Canada and into the northeastern states. Blooms early spring into early summer. FACTS/USES: The genus *Arabis* is named after Arabia. The plant has a very pungent or acrid taste, and it is considered unpalatable for livestock and humans.

FEW-SEEDED DRABA   *Draba Oligosperma*

This small, densely tufted perennial grows from a half inch to four inches tall. The linear leaves have a prominent midvein and are densely overlapped. Minute hairs cover the leaves and, examined with a hand lens, the hairs are pinnately branched, like two combs back to back. The leafless stems rise slightly above the clump and bear several bright yellow, four-petaled, cross-shaped flowers that fade to pale yellow as they mature. The fruit is a short, ovoid pod, nearly a quarter of an inch long, and smooth or sometimes pubescent. HABITAT/RANGE: Few-seeded draba is a widespread species found on dry sunny cliffs from plains and foothills to alpine ridges. It is distributed from Alaska to Colorado, Nevada and central California. Blooms early spring to midsummer, depending on elevation. FACTS/USES: The specific name means few-seeded. Drabas are a difficult group to identify without a mature fruit and technical characters of the hairs.

ROUGH WALLFLOWER   *Erysimum asperum*

The cluster of bright yellow to orange flowers are arranged on a branched raceme. The flower buds at the base of the cluster bloom first, then flower upward. As the flowers mature, a long four-sided, one- to five-inch, upward-pointing pod or silique forms. The narrow and linear leaves are clumped at the base and follow the six- to 36-inch stem. HABITAT/RANGE: Rough wallflower is common on open hillsides, flats and road cuts, from plains into the montane zone. It is found from British Columbia to central Canada, south to Texas and west to southern California. Blooms during late April to July. FACTS/USES: Its generic name, *Erysimum*, is derived from the Greek word, *erusimon*, meaning to draw, as some species in the genus were used to cause blistering. Its specific name, *asperum*, means rough and refers to the minute hairs or pubescence on the stem and leaves.

PAYSON'S BLADDERPOD   *Lesquerella paysonii*
Bladderpods are fairly easy to identify as a group. They all are rosette-forming plants with four-petaled, yellow flowers in loose, short racemes. Fruits are small, inflated, ovoid-shaped, bladderlike pods. The most distinguishing feature as a group are the stellate (star-shaped) hairs covering the entire plant, but you cannot appreciate these hairs without a microscope. The stems generally arise from a rosette of silvery ovate-shaped leaves. HABITAT/RANGE: Occurs sporadically in the drier, rocky talus slopes and windswept ridges and is limited in range to western Wyoming and Idaho. One of the earliest flowers to bloom on open, south-facing slopes in early spring. FACTS/USES: The genus name of this group was named for Leo Lesquereux (1805-1889), an American bryologist—one who studies bryophytes, including true mosses, peat mosses and liverworts.

WATERCRESS   *Nasturtium officinale*
Watercress is a floating aquatic plant with creeping, prostrate stems that root at the nodes, allowing the plant to anchor itself in shallow water or mud flats. The bright green, three to nine segmented leaflets and shoots form a dense, tangled mass along stream banks. The flowers are small and white, in dense to elongate racemes. The fruit is a slender, curved silique up to one inch long. HABITAT/RANGE: A widely distributed European species that has established itself in springs and slow streams throughout the United States, watercress blooms from early spring until late fall. FACTS/USES: Watercress is a well-known addition to salads. The leaves give salad a mild peppery taste. Ancient Greeks and Romans used this plant in a number of ways: They used the seeds as an aphrodisiac, burned the leaves to neutralize scorpion venom, and it was considered good food for deranged minds.

ALPINE SMELOWSKIA   *Smelowskia calycina*
This low, gray, cushion-forming perennial plant has persistent old leaves on the caudex. The pinnate leaves are mostly clustered at the base—basal leaves have stiff hairs on the petioles—with smaller leaves along the stem. The white or cream to purplish-tinged flowers are arranged in a dense raceme at the end of the two- to eight-inch stem. The fruit is an erect, linear silique a half-inch long. HABITAT/RANGE: A widespread plant inhabiting subalpine to alpine moraines, windswept ridges and rocky crevices of eastern Asia and western North America, extending south to Colorado. Flowers during early summer into August. FACTS/USES: The genus was named after an 18th-century Russian botanist, Timotheus Smelowsky. This wildflower grows during the short summer season of the high alpine. Under extreme, harsh conditions, this plant is stunted but, when protected from harsh elements, it produces robust flowering stems.

FIELD PENNYCRESS   *Thlaspi arvense*

An annual or winter annual, this weedy herb rises four to 20 inches high. The single or branched stem is glabrous and erect. The leaves are narrow and obovate, either entire or finely toothed. The lower leaves are petioled, and the upper leaves clasp the stem. The white, four-petaled flowers are in racemes. The seed capsules (silicles) are the distinguishing feature of this plant. They are orbicular to obcordate in shape, notched, wing-margined with two to eight seeds per locule, and the seed capsules are persistent throughout the summer. HABITAT/RANGE: This introduced weedy plant from Europe has spread throughout North America, and is common in lower elevations, especially in disturbed fields and roadsides. Blooms early spring to early summer, while moisture is available. FACTS/USES: The specific name means pertaining to cultivated fields.

Stonecrop Family

Crassulaceae

LANCELEAVED STONECROP   *Sedum lanceolatum*

Easily identified by thick succulent leaves, each flower is congested on the end of a three- to six-inch stem and has five sharp, pointed petals resembling a bright yellow star. HABITAT/RANGE: Found from sea level to alpine tundra, it is perhaps one of the most common wildflowers in the Northern Rockies. Blooms during late June to August on open, dry sites with gravelly to rocky soils. FACTS/USES: The Latin generic name is derived from *sedeo*, meaning to sit, in reference to its low-growing habit. To adapt to dry conditions, it has developed a system for water conservation. On the leaf surface of highly evolved plants are minute pores called stomata. Stomata allow carbon dioxide to enter and water vapor to escape for the process of photosynthesis. To prevent water from escaping during the hot part of the day, the stomata close. During the night, they open to allow carbon dioxide to enter, storing it for daytime use.

ROSE CROWN   *Sedum rhodanthum*

Rose crown is an erect plant, four to 15 inches tall, arising from stout rootstocks. The stems usually are clustered and unbranched, with numerous, fleshy, flattened stem leaves. At the top of a stem is a dense cluster of rose-colored flowers. The small flowers are arranged in close racemes in the axils of the upper leaves. HABITAT/RANGE: Rose crown is found primarily in wet or springy places or among rocks of montane habits, but usually is in subalpine and alpine habitats. Distributed from central Idaho and Montana, south to New Mexico and Arizona. Blooms sometime between late June and mid-August. FACTS/USES: *Rhodanthum* is Greek for rose-flowered. Most of the *Sedums* are edible, especially as new shoots or young leaves. As they age, they become bitter. Adding the leaves to salads is their most common use.

KING'S CROWN   *Sedum roseum*

King' Crown is a perennial plant with succulent leaves. Small deep purple or maroon flowers are clustered on the end of a one- to 12-inch stem. Plants are unisexual, with staminate (male) and pistillate (female) parts on separate plants. HABITAT/RANGE: Widely distributed in Eurasia and North America. Found along the Rockies to New Mexico, and prefers subalpine to alpine—moist, cliff, talus slope or open ridge—areas. Blooms in early summer. FACTS/USES: The specific name, *roseum*, means rose or rosy and may refer to the roselike fragrance of the root. The young leaves and shoots of this herb can be used as a salad plant or potherb. King's Crown is, however, considered an emergency food and should not be taken in more than moderate amounts. As the leaves become mature, the taste becomes more acidic and bitter.

Saxifrage Family
Saxifragaceae

ROUNDLEAF ALUMROOT   *Heuchera cylindrica*

It is a herbaceous perennial that rises six to 30 inches from a thick, woody rootstock. The leathery, ovate or heart-shaped leaves are clustered at the base on long or short petioles. The cream or greenish, cup-shaped flowers are clustered in a narrow, spikelike raceme. The upper portion of the flower stalks are densely covered with glandular hairs. HABITAT/RANGE: Alumroot inhabits moist to dry, sunny, rocky hillsides, cliffs and talus slopes of montane to above timberline. A cordilleran species found from British Columbia to Alberta, western Wyoming, northern Nevada and northeastern California. Blooms from April to August, depending on elevation. FACTS/USES: The specific name means cylindrical-spiked. Alumroot has several medicinal uses: It is an astringent for healing sores, a rectal injection for intestinal disorders, and the roots are eaten raw for mild diarrhea.

WOODLANDSTAR   *Lithophragma parviflora*

Woodlandstar is a slender, glandular-pubescent, perennial herb with a bulblet-bearing rootstock. The leafy, flowering stems attain a height of three to 15 inches. Most of the roundish, deeply cleft, palmate-like leaves are basal with smaller stem leaves. Several white, starlike flowers—each of the five petals having three lobes—terminate on the stem in a raceme. The fruit is a three-valved capsule. HABITAT/RANGE: A rare and local wildflower of sagebrush and grassland foothills to lower montane forests, woodlandstar is distributed from British Columbia, Alberta to the Dakotas, south to Colorado and northern California. Flowers during spring and early summer. FACTS/USES: The generic name is derived from the Greek word, *lithos*, for stone, and *phragma*, for wall, referring to its preferred niche. The specific name, *parviflora*, means small-leaved.

FIVE-STAMENED MITREWORT   *Mitella pentandra*
A small perennial herb with creeping rootstocks, the four- to 16-inch stems usually are leafless, or there are one or two foliate leaves near the base. The basal leaves are roundish, with crenate margins and long petioles. The white or greenish flowers are arranged in a simple raceme. Each flower has five rectangular sepals alternating with five stamens and five comblike or feather-like petals twice the length of the sepals. The fruit is a two-valved capsule containing small, shiny, blackish seeds. HABITAT/RANGE: This plant prefers moist stream banks or wet meadows of woodlands or coniferous forests from montane to near timberline. A cordilleran species found from Alaska to Alberta, south to Colorado and central California. Flowers June to early August. FACTS/USES: The name mitrewort is derived from the Latin word *mitra*, and refers to the fruit shape.

FRINGED GRASS-OF-PARNASSUS   *Parnassia fimbriata*
This small, tufted, perennial herb ascends four to eight inches from rootstocks. Most of the kidney-shaped, long petioled leaves are basal, except for a small, bract-like leaf midway up the stem. A single, white, saucer-shaped flower terminates on each stem. Each flower has five petals, fringed at the base, with five fertile stamens alternating with five gland-tipped sterile stamens. The fruit is a many-seeded, four-valved capsule. HABITAT/RANGE: This plant prefers wet or boggy stream banks or meadows of montane or alpine zones. Commonly found from Alaska to Alberta, south to New Mexico and central California. Flowers July to mid-August. FACTS/USES: Its name is derived from Mt. Parnassus, Greece, the sacred mountain of the Muses, who were the nine daughters of Zeus. Each daughter presided over a different art or science. The specific name, *fimbriata*, means fringed.

BROOK SAXIFRAGE   *Saxifraga odontoloma*
This brook-loving saxifrage has leafless flower stems arising from a mass of shiny, round, deeply indented or toothed, margined leaves. The stems usually are between eight and 24 inches tall and support an open inflorescence of small white or pinkish flowers. Each flower has five roundish petals with 10 conspicuous, red, spreading stamens. HABITAT/RANGE: Found along moist, mossy streambanks and wet meadows from lower montane to alpine habitats. Widely distributed from Alaska to Alberta, south to northern New Mexico and Arizona. Blooms mid- to late summer. FACTS/USES: The species name *odontoloma* means sharp-toothed. Brook saxifrage easily can be confused with red-stemmed saxifrage *(Saxifraga lyallii)*, though red-stemmed saxifrage generally is less than eight inches tall and has a smaller, more closed inflorescence.

WESTERN SAXIFRAGE   *Saxifraga occidentalis*
Western saxifrage is a perennial woodland wildflower. It grows in small clumps with basal, coarsely toothed, ovate or triangular leaves that taper to a long or short petiole. An erect, reddish, slightly glandular-hairy stem ascends two to 15 inches from the clumps. Each stem bears 10 or more small, white or cream-colored flowers in a diffuse or congested branched pancile. The flowers have five ovate or oblong petals, 10 stamens with slender or club-shaped filaments and a two-chambered, nearly separated, ovary. HABITAT/RANGE: This plant dwells amid wet riparian stream banks, moist meadows and rocky cliffs. It is distributed from British Columbia to Alberta, south to western Wyoming, northern Nevada and Oregon. Flowers April to August. FACTS/USES: *Occidentalis* means Western. This species is highly variable and difficult to distinguish from other saxifrages.

PURPLE SAXIFRAGE   *Saxifraga oppositifolia*
Purple saxifrage, a perennial, forms a dense mat, only two to three inches tall, with somewhat woody trailing branches. The leaves are small—one-eighth-inch long, opposite, four-ranked, overlapping, with stiff, bristly hairs along the edge. Each short, leafy stem bears a single, bright purple-lavender flower, each of which is comprised of five petals and 10 stamens. This is the only species in the Saxifrage genus of our region with purple flowers; all others are white, yellow or red. HABITAT/RANGE: A common wildflower above timberline on alpine mountain slopes or arctic tundra in damp gravelly soils and rocky ledges. It is a circumpolar species found as far south as Oregon and Wyoming. Blooms June to August. FACTS/USES: The specific name means opposite-leaved. The generic name is a Latin derivative from *saxum*, meaning rock, and *frangere*, to break.

JAMES' SAXIFRAGE   *Telesonix jamesii*
This subalpine flower has one or several short two- to eight-inch stems that arise from a basal clump of heart- or kidney-shaped leaves. Each leaf is generously toothed and lobed. The pink to reddish-purple flowers are clustered in an elongated inflorescence. Each flower has five rounded, widely spaced petals that are attached by slender stalks to the lip of a reddish-purple, bell-shaped calyx. Leaves and stems are covered with purplish glandular hairs. HABITAT/RANGE: James' saxifrage is a dweller of moist, rocky crevices, north-facing exposures, and talus slopes—especially limestone—of subalpine and low alpine zones. It occurs along mountain ranges from Alberta to South Dakota, south to Colorado, Utah and southern Nevada. It can be found blooming during July and August. FACTS/USES: The common and specific name honors Edward James, a 19th century naturalist.

Hydrangea Family
Hydrangeaceae

MOCKORANGE   *Philadelphus lewisii*

Mockorange is a very showy, erect to spreading deciduous shrub four to 10 feet tall. The white, four-petaled, numerous yellow-stamened flowers are clustered at the ends of short branches. The one-inch-wide flowers emit a sweet, fragrant smell, reminiscent of orange blossoms. The leaves are opposite, ovate, and entire or with small serrations. The fruit is a woody capsule. This flower can be confused with Pacific dogwood *(Cornus nuttallii)*. HABITAT/RANGE: It prefers rocky hillsides, cliffs, talus slopes and streams banks of sagebrush deserts to Douglas-fir forests. Distributed from British Columbia to western Montana, central Idaho to central California. An early spring bloomer. FACTS/USES: The generic name is derived from the Greek word *philos*, meaning love, and *delphos*, for brother, and honors Ptolemy Philadelphus, third-century B.C. king of Egypt. Mockorange is the state flower of Idaho.

Gooseberry Family
Grossulariaceae

SQUAW CURRANT   *Ribes cereum*

This plant is a highly branched, glabrous to pubescent, unarmed, perennial shrub two to six feet tall. The pink to whitish flowers, a quarter- to a half-inch long, have a five-lobed calyx tube fused to the ovary, and the petals are inserted inside the tube. The leaves generally are three- to five-lobed, toothed and palmately veined. The fruit is a berry, about a quarter- to a half-inch in diameter, globe-shaped, smooth, and dull to bright red. HABITAT/RANGE: It prefers moist soils of sunny hills, ridges, slopes and clearings of foothills to montane zones. It is distributed from British Columbia to Montana, Nebraska, Colorado, New Mexico and southern California. Blooms spring to early summer. FACTS/USES: This species of currant is considered unpalatable and has an insipid taste. It can be used as an emergency food but caution must be taken.

MOUNTAIN GOOSEBERRY   *Ribes montigenum*

Mountain gooseberry is a small, spreading shrub, growing to only three feet tall. It branches freely, and the stems are bristly with sharp spines at the nodes. The leaves are strongly pubescent and glandular on the surface and are three- to five-lobed and toothed. Three to eight small, green, pink or purplish, saucer-shaped flowers droop in a raceme stemming from the leaf axils. The fruit is a purplish, densely granular-bristly berry and is edible. This species is very similar to swamp gooseberry *(R. lacustre)*, the primary difference being that the leaves of *R. lacustre* are glabrous and shiny. HABITAT/RANGE: Mountain gooseberry is primarily a subalpine to alpine species found on talus slopes and rocky bluffs. Well-distributed from British Columbia to Montana, south to New Mexico and southern California. FACTS/USES: The specific name means mountain-born. As a general rule, gooseberries have spines, while currants do not.

STICKY CURRANT   *Ribes viscosissimum*

Sticky currant is a bushy, spineless shrub with sticky upper twigs and reddish, shreddy bark on the older stems. The leaves, young shoots, flowers and berries usually are densely glandular-hairy and sticky to the touch. The somewhat rounded leaves are shallowly and palmately three-lobed and irregularly toothed. Greenish to dull white, tubular flowers, tinged with pink, are borne in corymbose racemes arising from the leaf axils. The fruit is a black, somewhat dry berry, covered with glandular hairs and tipped with withered flower parts. HABITAT/RANGE: Sticky currant is a mountain species of moist or dry, open to heavily timbered, especially rocky, slopes. It is well-distributed from British Columbia to northern Montana, south to Colorado and California. Blooms from May to July, with fruit developing in August and September. FACTS/USES: The specific name means sticky.

Rose Family
Rosaceae

SERVICEBERRY   *Amelanchier alnifolia*

Serviceberry is a large, bushy shrub two to 20 feet tall, with bright white flowers. The stems and twigs are dark gray or reddish, with alternate dark green leaves. The leaves are up to two inches long, elliptic and distinctly toothed above the middle. The showy flowers are clustered near the end of branches and have five strap-like petals with numerous yellow stamens. The fruit is a sweet, dark purple, berrylike pome. HABITAT/RANGE: It is found on dry to moist, rocky slopes and open woods. It is one of the most widely distributed shrubs in the West, from Alaska to Alberta and south. Flowers spring and early summer. FACTS/USES: The name serviceberry originates in the Appalachian Mountains. During the winter, roads were impassable for the circuit-riding preachers. In May, when the roads opened, it coincided with the blossoms, which became known as "service-time berries."

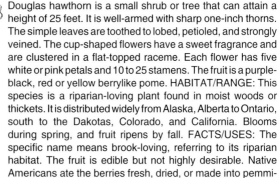

DOUGLAS HAWTHORN   *Crataegus douglasii*

Douglas hawthorn is a small shrub or tree that can attain a height of 25 feet. It is well-armed with sharp one-inch thorns. The simple leaves are toothed to lobed, petioled, and strongly veined. The cup-shaped flowers have a sweet fragrance and are clustered in a flat-topped raceme. Each flower has five white or pink petals and 10 to 25 stamens. The fruit is a purple-black, red or yellow berrylike pome. HABITAT/RANGE: This species is a riparian-loving plant found in moist woods or thickets. It is distributed widely from Alaska, Alberta to Ontario, south to the Dakotas, Colorado, and California. Blooms during spring, and fruit ripens by fall. FACTS/USES: The specific name means brook-loving, referring to its riparian habitat. The fruit is edible but not highly desirable. Native Americans ate the berries fresh, dried, or made into pemmican.

WHITE DRYAS   *Dryas octopetala*

White dryas is a dwarf, mat-forming shrub. The prostrate, trailing branches root freely, and the stems are leafy with dried persistent leaves. The dark green leaves are leathery, wrinkled, lanceolate, coarsely serrated on the margins and whitish-hairy on the underside, giving the leaf a two-tone appearance. Each erect, two- to 10-inch stem bears a single, large, white flower with eight to 10 petals and numerous stamens. The persistent styles elongate into long plumes and are feather-like in appearance. HABITAT/RANGE: Prefers wet, gravelly, or stony soils of high montane or above timberline. Well-distributed from Alaska to Labrador, and in the Rocky Mountains, south to Colorado and northeast Oregon. Flowers July through August. FACTS/USES: The specific name means eight-petaled. This shrub has many adaptations for its high, cold environment.

WOODS STRAWBERRY   *Fragaria vesca*

Woods strawberry is a low, perennial herb that spreads by stolons or runners. The plant ascends from a scaly rootstock, producing a small, basal clump of compound leaves. The leaves have three coarsely toothed leaflets that generally are bright yellow-green and prominently veined. The flowers are borne in small clusters and have five white petals and 20-25 stamens. The aggregate fruit is red, fleshy and juicy. Another related species *(F. virginiana)* is differentiated by glaucous, bluish-green, thick and not prominently veined leaves. HABITAT/RANGE: An inhabitant of moist meadows, stream banks and open woods. Widely distributed throughout temperate North America, Europe, Asia and South America. Blooms in spring and early summer. FACTS/USES: *Vesca* means weak or feeble. The berries are sweet and delicious raw or cooked into jams, jellies or syrups.

LARGE-LEAVED AVENS   *Geum macrophyllum*

Large-leaved avens is a delicate-looking plant that grows up to three feet tall with several stems and a few small half-inch, bright yellow flowers on delicate branches at the top. The flowers become rounded seed heads. *Geums*, or avens, are very similar to cinquefoils *(Potentilla)*. But *Geum's* style is jointed and bent near the center, and its pinnately compound leaves have a few large, one-inch leaflets that are narrow at the base and broad at the tip. HABITAT/RANGE: This moist, mountain meadow and woodland flower is found from Alaska to the Dakotas, south to northern New Mexico and Baja California. Flowers late May through July. FACTS/USES: The specific name means large-leaved. Other members of the *Geum*, specifically *rivale,* a northeast species, are known for their chocolate-like beverage brewed from the rootstocks.

ALPINE AVENS   *Geum rossii*

Alpine avens is a bright yellow flower reminiscent of cinquefoil or mountain buttercups, but the grayish, hairy leaves are pinnately divided into many narrow, irregular segments, helping to differentiate this species. The stems, ascending from rhizomes, rarely exceed one foot in height and bear one to four flowers. Like most alpine plants, this species often forms a dense cluster. HABITAT/RANGE: This plant is a dweller of moist soils in alpine meadows and rocky crevices. It is a cordilleran species, found from Alaska to New Mexico and Arizona, and also inhabits Asia. Because it is an alpine species, it blooms late in the season, from mid to late summer. FACTS/USES: As an adaptation to its alpine environment—which includes desiccating winds and intense solar radiation—this plant has a cover of fine gray hairs that acts both as an insulator and a filter.

PRAIRIE SMOKE   *Geum triflorum*

This plant is a tufted perennial ascending six to 20 inches from a stout rootstock. The leaves are mainly basal, covered with hairs and pinnately compound into fernlike segments. The pink or reddish bell-shaped flowers usually are borne three in a cyme and nod while in blossom. As the flowers mature, the stems become erect and the styles elongate into feather-like plumes. HABITAT/RANGE: This plant prefers dry to moist grasslands, sagebrush plains to subalpine meadows. It is distributed widely across southern Canada and the northern United States, south to New Mexico and central California. Flowers from spring to midsummer. FACTS/USES: The specific name means three-flowered. The common name, prairie smoke, refers to the cluster of reddish, plumose styles, which have the appearance of a puff of smoke. The boiled roots produce a tonic tea.

OCEAN-SPRAY   *Holodiscus discolor*

Ocean-spray is a bushy shrub with somewhat spreading branches; it grows from two to 15 feet in height. The stems are erect and the young twigs are finely hairy, while the older bark is grayish-brown. The alternate leaves are somewhat egg-shaped, with double-toothed margins. The upper surface is dark green and slightly hairy, while the lower surface is grayish or white-woolly. The small, numerous, cream-colored flowers form a dense terminal cluster or panicle. This plant easily can be confused with spireas. HABITAT/RANGE: It occupies a variety of sites—from moist, shady forests of coastal plains to low mountains and arid coniferous forests. It grows from British Columbia to western Montana, south to southern California. Flowers June to July. FACTS/USES: The specific name means two-colored or of different colors.

TALL CINQUEFOIL *Potentilla arguta*

This is a tall—usually more than 16 inches high—rather weedy-looking perennial herb with somewhat sticky glandular hairs on the stem and inflorescence. The leaves are pinnately divided into five to 11 leaflets, which are lobed, toothed and hairy. The pale yellow, cream or white flowers usually are crowded on a narrow cyme. While in bloom, the petals equal or slightly exceed the length of the sepals but, in fruit, the sepals enlarge and enclose the cluster of achenes. HABITAT/RANGE: It grows in rich, deep loams of moist meadows, along irrigation ditches and open hillsides, but not in alpine areas. It occurs from Alaska to Alberta, south along the mountain ranges to Utah and Arizona. Flowers May to July. FACTS/USES: The specific name means sharp-toothed. Many species of cinquefoil have been used medicinally, mainly as an astringent.

SHRUBBY CINQUEFOIL *Potentilla fruticosa*

This is a diffusely branched shrub, which generally grows one to two feet tall but occasionally reaches five feet, under good growing conditions. The stem is woody, twisted and tough, with silky-hairy young stems maturing to shreddy, brown bark with age. Its leaves are grayish-green and pinnately divided into three to seven linear, leathery leaflets that are silky-hairy underneath. In blossom, the shrub produces a profusion of bright yellow, saucer-shaped, half-inch- to one-inch-diameter flowers. The seeds, or achenes, are small, numerous and densely hairy. HABITAT/RANGE: It has a wide altitudinal range, from foothills to subalpine slopes, but it prefers moist, cool climates. It is distributed from Alaska to Labrador, south to New Jersey, Pennsylvania, Minnesota, New Mexico and California, and Eurasia. Blooms through the summer. FACTS/USES: The specific name means shrubby or bushy.

SLENDER CINQUEFOIL *Potentilla gracilis*

Slender cinquefoil is an erect, bushy perennial herb ascending one to two feet from deep, woody taproots. The flowers are arranged in a loose, many-flowered cyme with small, leafy bracts at the base. Each saucer-shaped flower usually is a deep yellow, about one-quarter to one-half inch in diameter, with 20 stamens in three rows. The leaves are mostly basal and digitately compound usually into seven green, toothed leaflets. There are numerous *Potentilla* species and differentiation can be difficult. HABITAT/RANGE: It is common on dry, sandy, gravelly, or clay loams of grasslands, sagebrush deserts to moist mountain slopes at subalpine. Distributed widely from Alaska to Saskatchewan, south to New Mexico and Baja, California, it blooms in June and July. FACTS/USES: The Latin generic name is derived from *potens*, meaning powerful, in reference to its medicinal properties.

COMMON CHOKECHERRY   *Prunus virginiana*

Chokecherry is a leafy shrub or small tree that can grow up to 25 feet tall. The shiny, green leaves are elliptic, with a fine, toothed margin. Small, numerous, whitish or cream-colored flowers are clustered in a raceme at the ends of leafy branches. The flowers later develop into a dark purple or black, juicy, berrylike drupe. HABITAT/RANGE: It prefers sunny, moist sites, especially along stream or river courses, seeps, and canyons, in addition to well-drained sandy soils of hillsides and talus slopes. It is widespread throughout southern California and the United States. Flowers usually in May or June and fruits in August or September. FACTS/USES: Chokecherry is edible, but it does pucker the mouth. When ample sugar is added, it makes delicious jellies, syrup or wine. This species is in the cherry genus and, though the seeds are nutritious, they, like peach pits, contain cyanogenetic poison.

ANTELOPE BITTERBRUSH   *Purshia tridentata*

This is a widely branched, semierect, grayish-green shrub with small, bright yellow flowers. This long-living, drought-resistant species usually is two to six feet tall. The leaves and flowers are two identifying characteristics: The leaves are clustered, wedge-shaped, three-toothed, and green on the upper surface, with a grayish woolly under surface; the flowers are solitary on short branchlets but clustered on the outer branches. HABITAT/RANGE: This plant prefers well-drained, sandy, gravelly soils and southern exposures of arid plains, foothills, and mountain slopes. It is distributed widely from British Columbia to Montana, south to New Mexico and California. Blooms May to July. FACTS/USES: The specific name means three-toothed. The common name is appropriate because the foliage has a very bitter taste. It is one of the most important Western browse plants for game animals.

WOOD'S ROSE   *Rosa woodsii*

Wood's rose is an erect, trailing or climbing shrub one to six feet tall. The stems usually have prickles and alternate leaves with flat-winged stipules. Each leaf is pinnately compound into five or seven leaflets that are elliptic and sawtooth-margined. The flowers—comprised of five heart-shaped petals and numerous yellow stamens—are showy, fragrant and red or pink in color. The fruit, or hip, is orange-red, with long tapering sepals. HABITAT/RANGE: It is abundant in moist sites of dry habitats, especially along riverbanks, canyons and open woods of lowlands and foothills. It occurs from British Columbia to Montana, south to Texas and southern California and in areas of Wisconsin and Kansas. Flowers May into July. FACTS/USES: The rose hips are edible and known for their concentration of vitamin C. The hips can be eaten raw, stewed or cooked into jams and jellies, with sugar.

RED RASPBERRY   *Rubus idaeus*

Wild red raspberry is similar to our cultivated garden variety, but smaller. This perennial shrub is strongly armed with prickles, especially near the base of the stem. The compound leaves have three to five sharply toothed leaflets. The white five-petaled flowers are in terminal or axillary clusters and mature into dark red, aggregate berries. HABITAT/RANGE: Inhabits wet or dry woods along mountain trails and rocky slopes. A native shrub over much of temperate North America and Eurasia. Blooms May through June, and produces fruit mid-July to September. FACTS/USES: Raspberries are excellent eaten raw or cooked into jams or syrup. Boiling the leaves for 20 minutes can produce a tea. The simmered roots have a number of medicinal uses—an eyewash, a treatment for weak lungs, a general tonic, and a relief for summer diarrhea.

THIMBLEBERRY   *Rubus parviflorus*

A plant very similar to red raspberry *(R. idaeus)* but more robust, with large, deep-green leaves up to 10 inches wide and three- to five-lobed. The stems are unarmed, lacking prickles. The white flowers are cup-shaped and mature to red aggregate berries, which taste rather dry and insipid. HABITAT/RANGE: Thimbleberry grows in moist to dry wooded to open sites, from sea level to the subalpine zone. It is well-distributed throughout the West, from Alaska to the Great Lakes and south to Montana, New Mexico and southern California. Blooms late May to July, with berries ripening July to September. FACTS/USES: The generic name means small-flowered. The berries are a special favorite of wildlife. The telltale red-stained droppings left on rocks and limbs by birds and other small animals indicate that ripe thimbleberries are not far away.

MOUNTAIN ASH   *Sorbus scopulina*

This shrub or small tree reaches three to 15 feet in height. The leaves are large, alternate and pinnately divided into 11 to 17 elliptic, finely serrated leaflets. The small, cream-colored flowers are borne in terminal, flat-topped clusters. The flowers mature by late summer or early fall into a cluster of glossy, bright orange or scarlet berrylike fruits, which usually persist into the winter. HABITAT/RANGE: Mountain ash often is found in moist soils of canyons and mountain hillsides. It is distributed from Alaska to western Alberta, south to the Dakotas, Wyoming, New Mexico and northern California. Flowers from May until early July. FACTS/USES: The specific name means of the rocks, referring to its habit of establishing in rocky canyons and hillsides. The bitter berries are edible raw, cooked or dried, but are a bigger attractant for birds—especially cedar waxwings—than for humans.

SHINY-LEAF SPIREA   *Spirea betulifolia*

Shiny-leaf spirea is a deciduous, erect shrub, one to three feet tall, arising from creeping rootstocks. It has rather oblong, birch-like leaves. The flowers are very small, less than one-eighth-inch long, with five sepals and five petals, and numerous protruding stamens. The white or pinkish-tinged flowers are densely arranged on a showy, flat-topped corymb. HABITAT/RANGE: This plant prefers deep, fertile and moist soils of open hillsides to dry woods. It occurs from British Columbia to Saskatchewan, South Dakota, Wyoming to Oregon, and also is found in Asia. Blooms early summer to midsummer. FACTS/USES: The generic name is derived from the Greek word *speira*, meaning spiral or coil, which may refer to the spirally twisted seed pods. The specific name means birch-leaved.

SUBALPINE SPIREA   *Spirea densiflora*

This is a low plant that grows up to three feet tall and is branched with dark, red-brown bark. It is distinguished easily by its dense cluster of tiny, red or pinkish flowers arranged in a flat-topped corymb. The leaves are elliptic, toothed, bright green on the upper surface and slightly puberulent on the lower surface. The fruit is a cluster of five seed pods (follicles) containing several small seeds. HABITAT/RANGE: As the common name implies, this species is a dweller of subalpine zones. It prefers rocky sites and often can be found growing in the soil-filled cracks of rocks. It is found from southern British Columbia to Montana, Wyoming and central California. Flowers early to midsummer. FACTS/USES: The specific name means densely flowered. Spireas have a reputed medicinal use as a general tonic made by brewing a tea from the stem, leaves or flowers.

Pea Family
Fabaceae

ALPINE MILK-VETCH   *Astragalus alpinus*

This is a low and matted perennial, four to 12 inches tall with lax, freely branched stems. The leaves are pinnately divided into six to 11 pairs of oblong or elliptic leaflets notched at the apex. Each leaflet has short, white bristly hairs underneath, with the upper surface smooth or with appressed hairs. Seven to 23 bluish, violet or sometimes white pealike flowers are arranged in a loose raceme. The pods are pendant, slightly inflated and conspicuously covered with brown or black hairs. HABITAT/RANGE: This species prefers the shade of wet areas along valley streambeds to above timberline. It is a circumboreal species found in North America, from northern Canada south to New England in the East, and New Mexico and northeast Nevada in the West. Blooms during midsummer. FACTS/USES: The specific name means alpine, and refers to its habitat. It can be poisonous if selenium is in the soil.

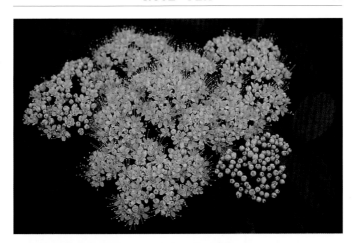

TWO-GROOVE MILK-VETCH   *Astragalus bisulcatus*
This tall, erect, many-stemmed perennial herb ascends one to two feet from woody taproots. The white to violet pealike flowers bend downward and are arranged in long, showy clusters or racemes. The leaves are pinnately divided into nine to 25 linear to elliptic leaflets, the upper surface of which are covered with fine, white hairs. The pendulous pods are nearly a half-inch long, with two grooves along the upper surface. HABITAT/RANGE: Typically occurs on alkaline soils of sagebrush deserts and grasslands. It is found mostly along the eastern slope of the Rocky Mountains, from Alberta to Montana, Nebraska and New Mexico. Blooms during May to August. FACTS/USES: The specific name means two-grooved. This species is one of the worst stock-poisoning plants in the West. It often grows on alkali soils where selenium is present and absorbs this poisonous element into the foliage. If selenium is absent, the plant is palatable.

THISTLE MILK-VETCH   *Astragalus kentrophyta*
Thistle milk-vetch forms a very low cushion or mat of spiny, stiff leaves. Small pealike flowers with purplish banners are partly hidden among the foliage, and each flower stem supports one to three flowers in a raceme. The leaves are pinnately divided into five to 11 linear to elliptic, silvery-strigose leaflets with sharp-pointed to spinose apexes. The small half-inch-long seed pod has one to four seeds. HABITAT/RANGE: This species inhabits a variety of habitats, from sandy deserts and badlands to alpine ridges and talus slopes. It is distributed from southern Alberta to the Dakotas, south to Nebraska, Colorado and central California. Flowers early to late summer. FACTS/USES: The *Astragalus* genus is a large group of diverse plants with some members having nearly identical appearance, making identification dependent upon technical features—usually the developed pods.

PURSH'S MILK-VETCH   *Astragalus purshii*
Pursh's milk-vetch is a low, tufted, grayish-green plant. The compound leaves are nearly the same length as the flowering stalks, giving the flowers, and later the pods, a nestled appearance among the leaves. The leaves are pinnately divided into seven to 10 round to acute leaflets, which are covered with dense gray hairs. The flower stalks bear three to 10 flowers on a raceme. Each pealike flower is white or yellow, with a reddish tinge on the inner petals. The pods are short, thick, curved and densely tomentose. HABITAT/RANGE: An inhabitant of clay and gravelly soils of sagebrush deserts to lower-mountain foothills, it is distributed from British Columbia to Alberta, south to the Dakotas, New Mexico and California. Flowers mid-April to July. FACTS/USES: The generic name is derived from the Greek word, *astragalos*, and means ankle bone, referring to the shape of the leaves or pod. It is a selenium accumulator.

FEW-FLOWERED MILK-VETCH   *Astragalus vexilliflexus*

Few-flowered milk-vetch is a low (less than one to two inches tall), prostrate, mat-forming perennial that grows from a thick taproot. It is branched profusely with small, pinnately compound, thinly haired leaves. Each leaf has seven to 13 leaflets with pointed—but not sharply pointed or lanceolate—tips. Each stem usually has several purplish, irregular flowers clustered along the stem on short stalks. It is confused easily with *A. kentrophyta*, which has lance-shaped leaflets. HABITAT/RANGE: Prefers stony subalpine slopes and alpine crests but is found lower into foothill habitat. It is distributed widely within its habitat along the eastern slope of the Rocky Mountains, from Banff National Park to Saskatchewan, Dakotas, south to Colorado. Flowers sometime between June and early July. FACTS/USES: The specific name, *vexilliflexus*, refers to its flexible, limber form.

AMERICAN LICORICE   *Glycyrrhiza lepidota*

American licorice is an erect, branching, perennial herb that ascends one to three feet from thickened rhizomes. The pinnate leaves are comprised of seven to 15 lanceolate leaflets. The yellowish-white flowers occur in dense racemes, which rise from the leaf axils. Later, the flowers will develop into burlike seed pods dotted with hooked spines. HABITAT/RANGE: Licorice usually is found in waste places, silty river bottoms and other moist, low ground. It is distributed widely throughout the West, from British Columbia to Ontario, south to Texas, New Mexico and California. Flowers June to early August. FACTS/USES: The generic name is derived from the Greek words, *glykys*, for sweet, and *rhiza*, for root. The specific name means with small scurfy scales and refers to the stalked glands covering parts of the plant. The sweet, pleasant-tasting roots can be eaten raw.

SWEETVETCH   *Hedysarum boreale*

Sweetvetch is a "bushy," highly branched perennial herb, one to two feet tall, with thin, brownish papery bracts or stipules at the base of each leaf. The leaves are pinnately divided into nine to 15 elliptic or oblong leaflets. Each leaflet is hairless, with minute brown dots or glands on the upper surface. The red to purplish-red pealike flowers are arranged in long, showy racemes. The fruit is a flattened pod, containing two to five seeds, with obvious constrictions between each seed. HABITAT/RANGE: This species grows on dry, clay soils of open or lightly shaded areas in sagebrush plains to aspen belts. It is distributed from the Yukon Territory to Newfoundland and south in our region to the Dakotas, New Mexico and Arizona. Blooms in late spring or early summer. FACTS/USES: The specific name means northern. Sweetvetch, unlike locoweed, is not poisonous, and the edible licorice-tasting roots have been used by Native Americans.

SILVERY LUPINE   *Lupinus argenteus*
Sky-blue flowers and somewhat gray, hairy foliage distinguish this lupine. Several varieties have been split from this species, and there is a wide variation in leaf size and shape, with leaflets ranging from oblanceolate to acuminate, and glabrous to densely grayish-hairy. The leaves are palmately divided into five to 11 leaflets and generally are bright green. Flowers are arranged in long spikes of small one-eighth- to one-inch pealike flowers. HABITAT/RANGE: This mountain flower of pine forests to subalpine ridges prefers moist soils. It is distributed from central Oregon to Alberta, to the Dakotas, south to New Mexico and northeast California. Flowers late June to early August. FACTS/USES: The specific name means silvery. Lupines are poisonous, especially the seeds, which contain alkaloids, but poisoning mostly is limited to domestic livestock.

SILKY LUPINE   *Lupinus sericeus*
Silky lupine is a perennial herb that grows in large clumps one to two feet high. It is distinguished by its pealike, light blue flowers, arranged in a dense terminal raceme, and its hairy or silky palmate leaves. HABITAT/RANGE: Silky lupine prefers dry soils of sagebrush deserts to lower montane forests. It is distributed widely from British Columbia to Alberta, south to New Mexico and California. Blooms June to early August. FACTS/USES: The specific name means silky. The name "lupine" is derived from the Latin name *lupinus*, meaning wolf. It was believed that lupines robbed the soil of its fertility, which is not true. On the roots are nodules with bacteria that fix nitrogen that otherwise would be lost. Nitrogen is an important element in the growth of all plants, and lupine actually provides extra nitrogen, thereby making the soil more fertile for other plants.

YELLOW SWEET-CLOVER   *Melilotus officinalis*
This is a tall, robust, highly branched biennial herb that grows up to 10 feet tall. The small, yellow, pealike flowers are arranged along a slender raceme. The leaves are divided into three lanceolate, finely toothed leaflets. A closely related species, white sweet-clover *(M. alba)*, is more widespread and important in the West but is not as noticeable as the bright yellow species. HABITAT/RANGE: Prefers waste and disturbed sites along roads and pastures. A native to Europe, it first found its way west with early missionaries and now is found over most of temperate North America. Flowers May to October. FACTS/USES: The generic name is derived from the Latinized form of an old Greek plant used by Aristotle around Sparta and Troy. The Greek word, *meli*, means honey, and *lotus* is a kind of wild clover. This species is a favorite of honeybees.

RABBIT-FOOT CRAZYWEED   *Oxytropis lagopus*
This small, tufted plant usually is covered with fine silky hairs. Lambert's crazyweed *(O. lambertii)*, a Great Plains species, is very similar in appearance. The distinguishing characteristic, however, is in the attachment of the silky hairs. Lambert's has hairs attached by their middle to a short stalk, while rabbit-foot has basally attached hairs. The bright rose-purple, pea-like flowers form dense racemes borne at the ends of leafless stalks. The leaves are pinnately divided into paired lanceolate leaflets. HABITAT/RANGE: This species typically occurs on well-drained sandy or gravelly soils of sagebrush plains to lower-mountain elevations. It is distributed from Idaho to Montana and south to Wyoming. Blooms mid-April to August. FACTS/USES: The generic name is derived from the Greek words, *oxus*, meaning sharp, and *tropis*, for keel, and refers to the sharp beak at the tip of the lowest two united petals, or keel, of the flower.

SILKY CRAZYWEED   *Oxytropis sericea*
Crazyweeds resemble many species of locoweeds *(Astragalus)*. They usually can be distinguished by their lack of stem leaves. This species is a perennial forb that arises three to 16 inches from a deep, woody taproot. White to yellowish pealike flowers are clustered in spikes at the ends of leafless, flowering stalks. The grayish-hairy leaves are basal, usually ascending from the rootcrown, and are pinnately divided into paired lanceolate leaflets. The fruit is a fleshy pod, which becomes hardened and bony as it matures. HABITAT/RANGE: It has a wide variety of habitats, from prairies to subalpine meadows and ridges. Silky crazyweed is distributed from British Columbia to central Idaho, northern Wyoming, south to Texas, New Mexico and Nevada. Blooms May to September. FACTS/USES: The specific name means silky. Extensive grazing of this species induces a chronic poisoning called locoism.

MOUNTAIN GOLDEN-PEA   *Thermopsis montana*
Mountain golden-pea is a perennial herb that ascends one to three feet from woody, creeping, underground rootstocks. The brilliant yellow, pealike flowers are borne in a dense, clustered raceme. The leaves are stalked and divided into three leaflets. A large, leaflike bract, or stipule, is at the base of each leafstalk. After the flowers mature, a one- to three-inch, dark-colored and densely hairy seed pod develops. A closely related species, *(T. rhombifolia)*, is very similar but does not grow as large and the seed pods generally curve into a ring. HABITAT/RANGE: Golden-pea grows in relatively dry soils but does best in moist bottomlands with rich loam soils of the montane zone. Ranges from Washington to Montana and south to New Mexico and northern California. Flowers late spring and early summer. FACTS/USES: The specific name means pertaining to the mountains.

LONGSTALK CLOVER
Trifolium longipes

This perennial herb ascends four to 12 inches and often is rhizomatous. Dense flower heads are borne on long stalks, which droop as the flowers age. The purple, pink or yellowish flower heads are composed of small pealike flowers about half an inch long. The leaves are palmately divided into three narrow leaflets one-half inch to three inches long. HABITAT/RANGE: Longstalk clover typically occurs in moist soils of wet meadows and along streams of lower montane valleys and meadows to subalpine slopes. It is distributed from Washington to Montana, south to New Mexico and California. Blooms late spring to midsummer. FACTS/USES: The specific name means long-stalked. Steeping the dried flower heads in hot water for a few minutes makes a flavorful and tonic tea. Other uses include medicinal use of the dried flowers for whooping cough and ulcers and use of the seeds for bread.

BIG-HEAD CLOVER
Trifolium macrocephalum

Big-head clover is a very low-growing clover with distinctive, large, round heads of deep pink and yellowish two-toned flowers. The flowers are one to two inches in diameter and are borne on the ends of slender, stout, three- to 10-inch stems. The leaves are palmately compound, with three to nine leaflets, which are oval-shaped, thick and have toothed margins. HABITAT/RANGE: Big-head clover prefers rocky soils of sagebrush deserts to ponderosa-pine woodlands. Distributed from central Washington to western Idaho and south to Nevada and east-central California, it flowers late April to June. FACTS/USES: The specific name means bearing large heads. The clovers can be eaten raw but are difficult to digest and can cause bloat. When cooked or soaked in saltwater for several hours, they can be eaten in quantity and are very nutritious and high in protein.

RED CLOVER
Trifolium pratense

Red clover is a perennial herb that lacks rootstocks and grows one to three feet tall. It has trifoliate leaves with broad, oval leaflets. The flowers are in heads or spikes and are composed of 50 to 200 small, pealike flowers varying from pink to purple. Bees are attracted to the red color and the fragrant blossoms, and clovers have an economic importance in the honey industry. The seed pods are small and usually contain a single, small, kidney-shaped seed. HABITAT/RANGE: Red clover often is found along roadsides, fields, fences and other disturbed sites of lowland to mid-montane elevations. Introduced from Europe, it has established itself throughout North America. Blooms throughout summer. FACTS/USES: The generic name means three-leaved. The specific name means of the meadows, referring to its preferred habitat. This species is the state flower of Vermont.

AMERICAN VETCH   *Vicia americana*

A smooth, trailing, or climbing perennial herb with three to nine pealike, bluish-purple flowers in a one-sided, loose raceme that originates from the axils of the leaves. The leaves are pinnately divided into eight to 14 hairless, oval or elliptic leaflets with the terminal leaflet developed into a tendril. The fruit is a hairless, two- to several-seeded, up to two-inch-long pod. HABITAT/RANGE: American vetch prefers rich, moist, clayey soils of plains and foothills to aspen belts, especially open, timbered areas with grassy meadows. This is a widespread native plant distributed from Alaska to Ontario, south to West Virginia, Missouri, Mexico and California. Flowers June to early August. FACTS/USES: The specific name means American and refers both to its wide distribution and the fact that it is the best-known of the native vetches. Like other legumes, this species possesses nodules containing nitrogen-fixing bacteria on the roots.

Geranium Family   **RICHARDSON'S GERANIUM**   *Geranium richardsonii*

Geraniaceae

Richardson's geranium is very similar in appearance and description to sticky geranium *(G. viscosissimum)*. In some high-mountain ranges, the two species actually hybridize. The main distinguishing characteristic is the white instead of pink flowers. The five-petaled white flowers have dark pink or purple veins—as does sticky geranium. These veins are nectary guides for pollinating insects. When the flower has been pollinated, the veins or lines usually fade. HABITAT/RANGE: This species often is associated with sticky geranium but prefers shady sites. It is distributed from British Columbia to Saskatchewan, south to New Mexico and California. A summer bloomer. FACTS/USES: Another common name for this plant is derived from the shape of the fruit. Crane's bill is an excellent description of the one- to two-inch-long beak. The genus name is a derivation of the Greek word *geranos*, meaning crane.

STICKY GERANIUM   *Geranium viscosissimum*

Sticky geranium is an abundant and conspicuous five-petaled, pink-lavender flower of the Rocky Mountain region. The specific and common name describes the honey-like stickiness of the upper stems and buds. Fine hairs have a glandular exudation on the ends, which also is responsible for the geranium smell. The plant has palmately cleft leaves, deeply divided into five to seven segments. It is a perennial herb that grows one to two feet tall and is highly branched, with numerous buds and flowers terminating on long stems. HABITAT/RANGE: This species prefers rich, moist loams of open woods and meadows of lowlands to montane. It commonly occurs from British Columbia to Saskatchewan, south to Colorado and California. A summer bloomer. FACTS/USES: The geranium house plant is in the same family as sticky geranium but in a different genus—*Pelargonium*. Only our wild geranium is a true geranium.

Flax Family
Linaceae

BLUE FLAX   *Linum perenne*

This plant produces fields of blue wild flax. It is a perennial species arising from a somewhat woody taproot to a height of six to 30 inches. The stems are rigid, with narrow, linear, sharp-pointed leaves, and bear several blue saucer-shaped flowers. Each flower has five petals and stamens, with the petals falling off soon after flowering. HABITAT/RANGE: Blue flax is found on dry, well-drained soils of prairies, foothills and alpine ridges. It is well-distributed across northern Canada and western North America. Flowers early spring to early fall, depending on elevation. FACTS/USES: The specific name means perennial. Flax has been an important cultural plant since the dawn of history. Linen thread, a strong fine fiber processed from the stems of the Old World flax *(L. usitatissimum)*, is used for weaving cloth and was used for binding Egyptian mummies. Flaxseed contains about 40 percent linseed oil.

Staff Tree Family
Celastraceae

MOUNTAIN LOVER   *Pachistima myrsinites*

Mountain lover is a small, evergreen shrub with glossy, leathery, opposite, oblanceolate leaves. The reddish-brown woody stems, up to three feet long, often spread or lie prostrate. At the leaf axils are clusters of small, numerous, maroon-colored flowers. Each flower is composed of four broad, persistent sepals and four petals attached under the edge of a flattened disk. The ovary is sunk in the disk. HABITAT/RANGE: This species often grows in moist, sandy or gravelly loams on coniferous northern slopes and prefers mid-montane forests. It occurs from British Columbia to Alberta, south to New Mexico and California. Flowers late spring to early summer. FACTS/USES: The specific name means myrsine-like, and refers to the resemblance to true myrtle of the Old World. The generic name is derived from the Greek words *pachys*, for thick, and *stigma*, hence the meaning thick stigma.

Spurge Family
Euphobiaceae

LEAFY SPURGE   *Euphorbia esula*

Leafy spurge is a perennial herb, one to three feet tall, that reproduces well from seeds or extensive rootstocks. The stems are erect and glabrous and, when injured, produce a milky juice. The leaves are alternate, broadly linear and usually droop. The distinguishing characteristic is the yellowish-green, heart-shaped, paired, leafy bracts subtending the small, greenish, cuplike flowers. HABITAT/RANGE: It grows in dense patches on disturbed sites, especially roadcuts, pastures and sandy banks. Introduced from Eurasia in the 19th century as a seed impurity, it since has established across southern Canada and the northern United States. Flowers early May throughout summer. FACTS/USES: The generic name honors Euphorbus, physician to King Juba II. Members of this family produce valuable products, such as rubber or latex and castor oil.

Sumac Family
Anacardiaceae

POISON IVY   *Rhus radicans*

Poison ivy is a woody shrub, up to six feet tall, or a vine that climbs via small aerial rootlets on the stems. The leaves are divided into three leaflets, which are egg-shaped in outline, coarsely toothed, shiny, and bright green, turning brilliant red in the autumn. The small, whitish-yellow flowers are clustered in a panicle—branching from the leaf axils—and are not very conspicuous. The fruit is a white berrylike drupe. HABITAT/RANGE: Poison ivy occurs mainly east of the Cascade Range to the Atlantic Coast and into Mexico—among streamside thickets, canyons and dry rocky hillsides of foothills to ponderosa forests. Flowers in early summer. FACTS/USES: All parts of this plant contain the toxin, urushiol, a yellow volatile oil that causes human skin irritation but does not affect grazing livestock. The standard external remedies usually contain ferric chloride.

Buckthorn Family
Rhamnaceae

SNOWBRUSH   *Ceanothus velutinus*

Snowbrush is a shiny, smooth, evergreen shrub, two to five feet tall. Its leaves are prominently three-veined, thick, dark green, shiny and sticky-resinous on the upper surface and pale velvety underneath. The common name, snowbrush, refers to the numerous clustered, white, fluffy flowers. Each small flower is composed of five sepals, five petals and five stamens. The seed capsules are glove-shaped, sticky-glandular and divided into three cells, each bearing a single seed. HABITAT/RANGE: Snowbrush is well-adapted to invade and establish in burned areas but prefers well-drained soils of pinyon-juniper belts up to aspen sites. It typically occurs from British Columbia to Saskatchewan, south to Colorado and California. Flowers early to midsummer. FACTS/USES: The specific name means velvety. The roots have nitrogen-fixing nodules that enrich the soil.

Mallow Family
Malvaceae

MOUNTAIN HOLLYHOCK   *Iliamna rivularis*

This large, herbaceous, perennial plant grows in coarse clumps with stems two to six feet tall. The leaves are maple-shaped, toothed and deeply three- to seven-lobed. The showy pinkish-white to rose-lavender flowers are clustered in loose racemes near the top of the stems. Flowers are one to two inches wide, with five petals and numerous stamens, fused at the base to form a tube around the branched style. HABITAT/RANGE: Found mostly in canyons or foothills near springs and along mountain streams in rich moist soil, it ranges from British Columbia to Montana and south to Colorado and Utah. Flowers June to late July. FACTS/USES: The specific name, *rivularis*, means brook-loving, referring to its streamside habitat. The fruit is a carpel, which splits into sections upon ripening. Each section contains three to four seeds.

SCARLET GLOBEMALLOW   *Sphaeralcea coccinea*
Scarlet globemallow is a low, grayish-green perennial herb with a cluster of red-orange or tomato-colored, five-petaled flowers. The gray appearance to the foliage is due to small, star-shaped hairs that can be seen with a hand lens. The leaves are deeply dissected or cleft into three to five lobes. HABITAT/RANGE: This plant grows in arid, sandy or gravelly soils of plains and foothills. Common on roadsides on the eastern slope of the Rocky Mountains, but ranges from Idaho to Alberta and as far east as Iowa, south to Arizona and Mexico. Blooms late April to mid-July. FACTS/USES: The Greek generic name, *Sphaeralcea*, is derived from *sphaera*, meaning sphere, and *alcea*, meaning mallow, referring to the globose fruit. The specific name, *coccinea*, means scarlet. In the spring, this flower dots the foothills with red.

St. John's Wort
Family
Hypericaceae

WESTERN ST. JOHN'S WORT   *Hypericum formosum*
This is a perennial herb ascending up to two feet tall from a thin, horizontal rootstock. Sessile, ovate-oblong leaves are opposite on a slender, erect stem. The foliage is purplish-dotted along the margins, but these spots are best observed against a light. Yellow flowers with five sepals and five petals are borne near the top in leaf axils, and buds appear reddish-tinged before opening. HABITAT/RANGE: It is a Rockies native and ranges from British Columbia to Montana, south to Mexico and Baja, California. Prefers moist sites, especially seeps and springs of midmontane to subalpine. Flowers June through September. FACTS/USES: *Formosum* means beautiful. Although no specific uses are attached to *H. formosum*, as a genera it occurs mostly in the subtropics and has medicinal uses. It does, however, contain hypericin, which causes photodermatis to those with sensitive skin.

COMMON ST. JOHN'S WORT   *Hypericum perforatum*
This is a perennial herb that bears several erect stems, one to three feet high. The opposite, lanceolate to elliptic leaves are covered with minute translucent dots. The showy, yellow flowers are starlike in appearance, with five petals, occasionally with black dots along the edge, and numerous, long stamens extending beyond the petals. HABITAT/RANGE: Common St. John's wort, introduced from Europe, has spread throughout North America. In the 18th century, it first established along the East Coast, then along the Pacific Coast north of central California, and now inhabits dry pastures and roadsides in the Rocky Mountains. Blooms June to September. FACTS/USES: The specific name, *perforatum*, means perforated. The plant is recognized as a poisonous range plant and causes skin irritations, especially to white-skinned animals.

BLUE VIOLET *Viola adunca*

Blue violet is a small compact plant, up to four inches tall, with miniature, bluish-violet, pansy-like flowers. Each flower is one-quarter-inch to one-half-inch long, with five petals. The lower petal extends backward into a slender spur. The dark green, ovate or heart-shaped leaves are basally clumped and arise on short stalks. HABITAT/RANGE: This species frequently is found along streams and the edges of subalpine meadows but also extends to lower elevations of dry to moist meadows, woods and open ground. Common throughout much of temperate North America, it is distributed in our region from Canada to the Great Plains and south to New Mexico and southern California. Flowers early spring to midsummer. FACTS/USES: The specific name means hooked, and refers to the slender, backward-projecting spur. The generic name, *Viola*, is an old Latin name for the genus.

CANADA VIOLET *Viola canadensis*

Canada violet is a small—six to 12 inches tall—freely branched, leafy stemmed species. The stems ascend from scaly rootstocks, and the flowering stalks rise from the leaf axils. The leaves are broadly heart-shaped, tapering to a slender tip, with the stem leaves progressively smaller and short-stalked. The flowers have five white petals with yellow at the base and often purplish-red on the reverse side. The three lower petals have purple nectary guides, or lines. HABITAT/ RANGE: This species, often found in dense patches, is a dweller of moist, shaded slopes, especially in rich aspen woods. It is distributed from Alaska to Alberta, south to New Mexico and Arizona, and through the central and eastern United States and Canada. Blooms May to July. FACTS/ USES: Violets have been used medicinally as a remedy for lung and skin diseases and as a blood purifier.

NUTTALL'S VIOLET *Viola nuttallii*

One of the first wildflowers to appear in the spring is the small yellow, pansy-like Nuttall's violet. When the flowers first emerge, they are nearly acaulescent, or lacking stems. Later, they develop leafy stems, five to 20 inches tall. The petals are decorated with purplish nectary guides or veins, and the back of the upper petals usually are reddish tinged. The leaves vary from oval to linear-lanceolate in shape and have long petioles. HABITAT/RANGE: This species inhabits rich moist soils of banks and open hillsides of prairies and woodlands to montane and subalpine zones. It is well-distributed, with several subspecies represented, throughout the Rocky Mountains. Flowers early spring to midsummer. FACTS/USES: The generic name honors Thomas Nuttall, a 19th-century naturalist and Harvard professor of botany, who traveled and collected specimens in the West.

Blazing Star Family
Loasaceae

TEN-PETALED BLAZINGSTAR   *Mentzelia decapetala*

This species usually is freely branched with shiny, silvery stems that attain one to four feet in height. The stems and leaves are covered with very fine, short, barbed hairs. The leaves are sessile and lance-shaped with long, deep cuts. As the common name implies, there are 10 whitish or pale yellow petals that open two to four inches, revealing as many as 200 showy stamens. The 10 petals help distinguish this plant from other species. HABITAT/RANGE: Ten-petaled blazingstar is found in dry, sandy or clayish soils of open plains, foothills and lower montane. It has a small distribution, typically occurring from Idaho to Alberta, south to Texas and Mexico. Flowers mid to late summer, with the blossoms opening at dusk and closing during the day. FACTS/USES: The specific name means 10-petaled. The ground-parched seeds make a nutritious meal.

BLAZINGSTAR   *Mentzelia laevicaulis*

Blazingstar is very similar in appearance to 10-petaled blazingstar. This species, however, has five brilliant, lemon-yellow petals that open into a star. The whitish stems are branched and have alternate, deeply cut or lobed leaves. Both stems and leaves are covered with fine, short, barbed hairs that give the plant a rough touch. HABITAT/RANGE: This species prefers dry soils of fine talus slopes and gravelly sagebrush plains of desert valleys to the lower montane. It often is a conspicuous flower on roadcuts. It occurs locally from southeastern British Columbia to Montana and south to Utah and southern California. Flowers late June to August and blooms mainly at night. FACTS/USES: The generic name honors C. Mentzel, a 17th-century German botanist. The specific name means smooth-stemmed.

Cactus Family
Cactaceae

CUSHION CORYPHANTHA   *Coryphantha vivipara*

Cushion coryphantha has globose or barrel-shaped stems, sometimes growing singly, but often forming clustered mounds. The spines are clustered and about a half-inch long. The waxy flowers have numerous petals and are reddish-purple in color. A plump, smooth, oblong, greenish fruit develops from the flowers. HABITAT/RANGE: It prefers dry, rocky or sandy soils of desert valleys and foothills. Cushion coryphantha is distributed from Alberta to Minnesota, Kansas, western Texas, northern Arizona and Oregon. Blooms late spring to early summer. FACTS/USES: The specific name means freely producing asexual propagating parts, referring to its ability to root and establish from a broken stem or joint. The generic name is derived from the Greek words *koryphe*, meaning cluster, and *anthose*, for flower, and refers to the numerous cluster blossoms.

BRITTLE CACTUS   *Opuntia fragilis*

Brittle cactus is made up of pads or joints, three to six inches long, growing in clumps. The pads are stems, not leaves, but they carry on photosynthesis for the plant. Under a thick layer of wax, the pads store moisture, enabling the cactus to withstand droughts and dry environments. The one-inch spines protect the plant from hungry animals. The showy flowers are yellow or greenish and waxy in appearance. HABITAT/RANGE: This species prefers dry, open ground, and is distributed from British Columbia to Wisconsin, south to Texas and California. Blooms late spring and early summer. FACTS/USES: The specific name means fragile or brittle. The Plains Indians regarded the cactus as an important plant in their lives. For them, its uses ranged from employing the pads in a children's tag game to extracting the juices to fix the colors painted on hides.

PLAINS PRICKLYPEAR   *Opuntia polyacantha*

The oval pads, or joints, of plains pricklypear are distinctly flattened and more firmly attached than its near relative, brittle cactus *(O. fragilis)*. The spines are only slightly barbed and the areoles are rusty-woolly. The waxy, yellow to reddish flowers produce dry to juicy, long, egg-shaped tan-colored fruits, full of seeds. HABITAT/RANGE: Occurs on open plains and foothills to lower mountain elevations. One of the most widely distributed of the flat-stemmed cactuses, it ranges from British Columbia to Alberta, south to Missouri, Texas and Arizona. Blooms late spring or early summer. FACTS/USES: The specific name means many-spined. Indians ate the fresh fruits and pads after the bristles were removed by burning. Chemical analysis of the pads indicates they are 80 percent water, with the remainder rich in minerals. Eating too much can cause scours.

Evening Primrose Family

Onagraceae

DEER HORN   *Clarkia pulchella*

This annual plant has distinctive four-petaled flowers that are deep rose-lavender. Each petal, about one inch long, has a broad three-lobed tip and a very narrow base, giving the petal a deer-antler appearance. All floral parts are arranged in fours, including four sepals fused together on one side of the flower; four fertile and four non-fertile stamens; a long style topped with a stigma comprised of four broad, generally white lobes; and a four-chambered inferior ovary. The plant usually attains a height of six to 20 inches with long, linear leaves along the stem. The fruit is an elongated capsule that splits open at maturity. HABITAT/RANGE: Prefers moderately dry, sandy, open areas—especially disturbed sites—of forests and foothills associated with sagebrush. It is distributed from British Columbia to Montana, south to Idaho and Oregon. Blooms early summer. FACTS/USES: The specific name means beautiful.

ALPINE WILLOW-HERB   *Epilobium alpinum*
This small, matted, perennial herb seldom exceeds a foot in height. The plant spreads by rhizomes or aerial runners, sending up one or more flowering stems to form a clump. Growing opposite along the stems are oval, nearly sessile, leaves. Small, white, pink or lavender flowers have four petals, each of which has a notch and two round lobes. The ovary is inferior and forms a dark brown or purple tube below the flower. This tube matures into a long, slender seed capsule. HABITAT/RANGE: The habitat requirement for this species is very specific, limited to moist banks, talus slopes and mountain meadows, often above timberline. It is a wide-spread, circumboreal species found from British Columbia to California. Commonly flowers from mid to late summer. FACTS/USES: The generic name is derived from Greek words *epi*, for upon, and *lobos*, for pod, referring to the inferior ovary.

FIREWEED   *Epilobium angustifolium*
Fireweed is a showy plant, two to six feet tall, with pink- to rose-colored, four-petaled flowers in a long, open spike. The blooms at the bottom open first and progress up the stem. As the flowers mature, they develop into long, slender seed pods. The stems usually are unbranched and leafy, with long lanceolate, prominently veined leaves. HABITAT/RANGE: Fireweed quickly establishes on disturbed soils in cool areas, from lower elevations to timberline. The plant often is found in spectacularly dense patches invading burned-over (hence, its common name) or cut-over areas. It is widely distributed from Alaska east to the Atlantic Coast and south to California. Blooms June to September. FACTS/USES: The specific name means narrow-leaved. The young shoots can be used as a potherb. Other uses include pounding the roots into a poultice to heal boils, reduce swelling, or relieve intestinal disorders.

EVENING PRIMROSE   *Oenothera caespitosa*
Evening primrose has a distinctive, large, white flower that grows close to the ground. The white flowers, two to four inches in diameter, have four heart-shaped petals, which turn pink or purple with age, and a four-lobed stigma. The plant is stemless, and the flowers and leaves arise from a root crown. Leaves are clustered, linear, two to six inches long, pinnately cleft and winged near the base. The inferior ovary develops into a woody, many-seeded capsule. HABITAT/RANGE: This species typically occurs on clay banks—often on red shale, talus slopes, road cuts and sandy soils of dry plains and foothills, into the ponderosa pine zone. It is distributed from Washington to Saskatchewan, south to the Dakotas, New Mexico and California. Flowers from late spring to midsummer. FACTS/USES: The specific name means tufted. It has a fragrant smell that attracts night-flying insects.

HOOKER'S EVENING PRIMROSE   *Oenothera hookerii*
This species attains a height of one to four feet and usually is unbranched. Long, lanceolate, plain to wrinkled margined leaves become progressively smaller upward along the stem. The four-petaled yellow flowers, which turn red or purplish as they age, are arranged in an elongated, terminal raceme interspersed with leafy bracts. The two- to three-inch-wide flowers are at the top of a one- to two-inch calyx tube of an inferior ovary and mature into slender, rigid capsules. HABITAT/RANGE: This common flower inhabits open slopes, road cuts and other disturbed, moist areas from the plains into the mountains at mid elevation. It is found from eastern Washington to Montana and south into western Texas and California. Blooms during mid to late summer. FACTS/USES: The Greek generic name is said to mean wine-scented. The root can be used as a potherb if used early in the season; it becomes bitter or peppery with age.

LONG-LEAVED EVENING PRIMROSE *Oenothera subacaulis*
Long-leaved evening primrose is a small, fleshy, taprooted perennial with long, lanceolate or oblong, dentate or entire margined leaves. The leaves and flower stems form a basal rosette. Flowers are four-petaled and yellow, with each petal about two-thirds of an inch long. Petals do not turn purple with age, as do *Oenothera flava* and *O. hookerii*. The eight stamens are unequal in length. HABITAT/RANGE: Limited in range from Washington to Montana, south into Colorado and Sierran California. Prefers open, drier meadows, streambanks and even disturbed sites. Blooms sometime between late May into July. FACTS/USES: The species name means somewhat stemmed. Roots (cooked), shoots (salad) and seeds of *Oenothera* species were known to be eaten by early Native Americans.

Bladderwort Family   **COMMON BLADDERWORT**   *Utricularia vulgaris*
Lentibulariaceae
Common bladderwort is a distinctive submersed aquatic plant with emergent flowering stems up to eight inches tall. Each stem bears six to 20, half-inch-long, bilaterally symmetrical yellow flowers. The leaves are finely divided into hairlike segments. Some of the segments are green and some have small, pale, transparent, buoyant bladders. The plant apparently is rootless or has only small fibrous roots. HABITAT/RANGE: Bladderwort is free-floating, often found in deep ponds and quiet lakes. Common throughout North America but not into the alpine zone. Blooms during summer. FACTS/USES: The specific name means common. The small, transparent bladders are thought to be insect traps. A narrow entrance lined with inward-pointing hairs allows tiny aquatic insects to enter but not to escape. Once inside, the trapped insects die and decompose, thus providing valuable nutrients and nitrogen for the plant.

Parsley Family
Apiaceae

SHARPTOOTH ANGELICA   *Angelica arguta*

Sharptooth angelica is an erect plant sending a thick, hollow stem two to five feet high from a taproot that is woody, thick and tends to have horizontal partitions in older plants. The large, pinnately compound leaves have long petioles with leafy sheaths at the base. Each leaf is comprised of numerous lance-shaped leaflets, sharp-tipped and bearing a sharp-toothed margin. The numerous small white flowers are borne in a compound umbel. When bruised, this plant emits an aromatic odor. This species is similar to, and often confused with, water hemlock (*Cicuta douglasii*). HABITAT/RANGE: Sharptooth angelica is found in moist areas of mountain meadows, on stream banks, and in shady woods from British Columbia to Alberta, south to Utah and California. Blooms July and August. FACTS/USES: The specific name means sharp-toothed. Angelica has many known medicinal uses, and Native Americans used the roots as good-luck charms.

WATER-HEMLOCK   *Cicuta douglasii*

This stout, perennial herb rises two to seven feet tall from a thick, tuberous root that is hollow and has prominent transverse partitions. The stems also are thick and hollow. The small white flowers are borne in compound umbels. The leaves are pinnately compound with lanceolate, saw-toothed-margined leaflets. This species can easily be confused with sharptooth angelica *(Angelica arguta)*. Two distinguishing characteristics of this species are that the veins of the leaflets terminate at the notches between the teeth and, when the foliage is bruised, it produces a musky odor. HABITAT/RANGE: Water-hemlock grows in wet, low places, especially in ditches and marshes where the roots are in water. It is a widespread cordilleran species. Flowers during June and July. FACTS/USES: This species is perhaps the most violently poisonous plant in the West. The toxin affects the nervous system.

HENDERSON'S CYMOPTERUS   *Cymopterus hendersonii*

Numerous bright green basal leaves spread outward from a taproot. The lower basal leaves may be long and linear, while central, stemmed leaves are pinnately divided two or three times into narrow segments. The leafless flowering stalks grow three to 12 inches tall and are topped with an umbel of bright yellow flowers and long narrow bracts extending beyond the flower clusters. Also has an aromatic carrot-like smell. HABITAT/RANGE: Prefers rocky open areas of foothills to above timberline. Limited in distribution from central Idaho to Montana (especially the Beartooth Mountains), south to northern New Mexico and northeastern Nevada. Blooms mid to late summer. FACTS/USES: The generic name is derived from the Greek words, *kyma*, meaning wave, and *pteron*, for wing, in reference to the winged fruits. The specific name honors pioneer Idaho botanist Lewis Henderson.

COW-PARSNIP   *Heracleum lanatum*
A robust perennial herb with hollow, jointed stems, up to eight feet tall, ascending from thick, woody, aromatic roots. Small white flowers are clustered on large, showy umbels, nearly a foot wide. The compound leaves are divided into three large, coarsely toothed leaflets, which are hairy or downy underneath. HABITAT/RANGE: Cow-parsnip thrives along stream banks, in wet bottoms or open woodlands. A widespread plant found from Alaska to Labrador, south to North Carolina, Texas and California. Flowers from June through July. FACTS/USES: Because of the plant's vigor and large size, the generic name is in honor of Hercules. The specific name means woolly, in reference to the hairy undersides of the leaves. Food uses include cooking the roots, which have a rutabaga taste. The roots also are reported good for rheumatism, digestion, and cramps. A salt substitute can be prepared from the thick, basal stems.

SWALE DESERT-PARSLEY   *Lomatium ambiguum*
This perennial herb ascends six to 24 inches from a thick, globose taproot. The leaves are compound and divided into narrow segments with the base of the petiole broadened and sheathing the stem. The small yellow flowers are borne in compound umbels. There are a number of Lomatium species; separating them is difficult and usually based on minute technical features. The bruised foliage of these plants produces a parsley-like odor. HABITAT/RANGE: This species prefers open slopes, flats and depressions of lowlands to the mid-montane. It is widespread from British Columbia to Montana, Colorado and Oregon. Blooms in early spring. FACTS/USES: The generic name, derived from the Greek word *loma*, refers to the winged fruit of this genus. The specific name means ambiguous. The fresh root of this species is edible and has a parsnip-like flavor; when dried, it has a distinctive celery-like taste.

DESERT-PARSLEY   *Lomatium dissectum*
Desert-parsley is a robust perennial herb that can obtain a height of one to five feet. The most distinguishing features of this species are the highly dissected leaves, which have a parsley- or fernlike appearance. Small yellow to purple flowers are borne in large compound umbels. The large taproot is fleshy and aromatic. HABITAT/RANGE: Desert-parsley often is found on open and rocky slopes and dry meadows of lowlands to mid-montane. Mainly distributed east of the Cascade Mountains from British Columbia to Montana, south to Colorado and northern California. An early spring and summer bloomer. FACTS/USES: The specific name means dissected or deeply cut. The roots were an important food source for Native Americans, who ate them raw, baked, roasted or dried and ground into flour, which they then made into bread or cakes—hence, another common name, biscuitroot.

GAIRDNER'S YAMPA   *Perideridia gairdneri*

A slender, branching perennial herb with delicate, narrow, pinnately compound leaves, which shrivel as the plant matures. Small white flowers are borne in umbels at the end of each branch. The one- to three-foot stems ascend from thickened, tuberous, carrot-like roots. HABITAT/RANGE: Gairdner's yampa grows on moderately moist soils in meadows and woodlands and on drier grassland and sagebrush sites from the lowlands to the montane. Dispersed through the central Rocky Mountains from British Columbia to Saskatchewan, south to Colorado and southern California. A late summer bloomer, which helps distinguish this species from *P. bolanderi*, an early summer bloomer. FACTS/USES: This was an important plant to the Native Americans. Yampa roots are nearly three inches long and are fleshy, with a sweet, nutty, carrot-like flavor when eaten raw. The seeds also can be used as an aromatic "caraway" seasoning.

Dogwood Family
Cornaceae

BUNCHBERRY DOGWOOD   *Cornus canadensis*

This colony-forming perennial herb grows four to 12 inches tall from a thin, scaly rootstock. The lower leaves are opposite, small and scaly; the upper leaves are broadly obovate and usually in a whorl of six. At the end of the stem, what appears to be a solitary white flower actually is an inflorescence—or cluster—of small, greenish to purplish flowers subtended by four large, white petallike bracts. The flowers later develop into a cluster of bright red, two-seeded drupe. HABITAT/RANGE: Bunchberry dogwood is a common wildflower of moist, open coniferous woods up to and above timberline. Widely distributed from Alaska to Greenland, south to Pennsylvania, Minnesota, New Mexico and California. Flowers during spring and early summer. FACTS/USES: The Latin name means horn or leather and may have referred to the knob of the roll on which manuscripts were kept. The fruit may be eaten raw or cooked.

RED-OSIER DOGWOOD   *Cornus stolonifera*

This willowlike shrub attains a height of three to eight feet and forms dense thickets. The reddish bark, which is brighter in the winter, is distinctive. The short-petioled, ovate-lanceolate leaves are opposite and have prominent pinnate veins. A cluster of small white flowers is borne in a flat-topped inflorescence. Each flower is comprised of four small sepals and four spreading, oval-shaped petals, four stamens and a club-shaped pistil. The fruit is a one-seeded, white or bluish berry. HABITAT/RANGE: This shrub typically occurs along stream banks and in damp ravines up to timberline, especially in association with willow. It is found from Alaska to Newfoundland, south to Pennsylvania, Missouri and Mexico. Blooms from May to July. FACTS/USES: The specific name means bearing stolons or runners that take root. Native Americans used the branches for baskets and the inner bark as a tobacco substitute and a tea.

Heath Family
Ericaceae

KINNIKINNICK   *Arctostaphylos uva-ursi*

Kinnikinnick is a low-trailing or matted, evergreen shrub, rarely more than two feet high, with long, flattened branches. The woody stems are brownish-red with flaky bark. The ovate leaves are leathery, shiny and dark green. Clustered in racemes at the ends of branches are small, waxy, pale pink, urn-shaped flowers, which later develop into bright red, pea-sized berries. HABITAT/RANGE: Kinnikinnick typically occurs on gravel or sand terraces, in coniferous woods, on dry banks and alpine slopes. It is a circumpolar species found in North America, from Alaska to Labrador, south to coastal California, New Mexico and the central and eastern United States. Flowers April to June. FACTS/USES: The common name, kinnikinnick, is a word used by Native Americans for tobacco mixtures. The specific name means bear's grape, referring to the fruits eaten by bears. The leaves have been used as a direuretic, for bronchitis, gonorrhea, and diarrhea.

PRINCE'S-PINE   *Chimaphila umbellata*

The most distinctive characteristics of this plant are its five-petaled, pinkish, saucer-shaped, nodding flowers. Ten stamens surround a prominent green ovary. The evergreen plant rises four to 12 inches from a branching rootstock. Arranged in whorls along the stem are leathery, waxy, elliptic leaves with saw-toothed margins. As the flowers mature into round-ish capsules, bearing numerous small seeds, the pedicels become erect and the fruits are held upright. HABITAT/RANGE: It commonly is found in coniferous woods and on alpine slopes where it is moist in the spring and dry in the summer. This circumboreal species is found in the Rocky Mountains, from Alaska to Alberta, south to New Mexico and California. Flowers from early to midsummer. FACTS/USES: The specific name means with umbels. The Greek generic name is derived from the words *cheima*, for winter, and *philos*, for loving, because of its evergreen habit.

ALPINE LAUREL   *Kalmia microphylla*

A small, low evergreen shrub that seldom grows to more than two feet in height. The leaves are leathery, lanceolate, smooth, dark green on the upper surface and whitish green on the lower surface, with rolled-under margins. The stems terminate in a corymb inflorescence with each flower on a long, slender, red pedicel. Each deep-pink-colored flower has five fused petals that form a bowl-shaped corolla. HABITAT/RANGE: Alpine laurel is primarily a subalpine or alpine plant, preferring wet mountain meadows and boggy sites. A mountain species distributed from Alaska to Alberta, south to Colorado and California. Flowers between June and September, depending on elevation. FACTS/USES: The specific name is in honor of Peter Kalm, an 18th century student of Linnaeus who collected plants in America. Alpine laurel is poisonous to grazing livestock.

SMOOTH LABRADOR-TEA   *Ledum glandulosum*
This moderately tall, stout, evergreen shrub obtains a height of two to five feet. Clustered at the tips of branches are bright white flowers with five petals and 10 protruding stamens. The oblong or oval leathery evergreen leaves are dark green on the upper surface and light-colored and dotted with tiny golden glands beneath. Flowers form a seed capsule on a recurving stalk with five cells, which split outward to disperse seeds. HABITAT/RANGE: Smooth labrador-tea is distributed from Alaska to British Columbia south to northwestern Wyoming and Sierra California, but it is mainly a Pacific Coast species. It typically occurs just below subalpine zones in acidic bogs or wet areas in the mountains. Blooms during July. FACTS/USES: The generic name means glandular, referring to the glands on the stems and leaves. Even though considered poisonous, a related species, *L. groenlandicum*, was used as a substitute for tea in the far North.

FOOL'S HUCKLEBERRY   *Menziesia ferruginea*
Fool's huckleberry may form dense thickets three to six feet tall. The erect shrub has deciduous, pale green, ovate leaves with waxy margins that form rosettes at the end of slender branches. Small pinkish urn-shaped flowers with four lobes hang by short stalks in clusters beneath the leaves. The fruit is a dry, inedible, four-parted capsule. Autumn foliage turns a brilliant crimson-orange. HABITAT/RANGE: Prefers shaded, moist coniferous forests and stream banks from Alaska to the Rocky Mountain states, south to California. Flowers during June and July. FACTS/USES: The generic name is in honor of Archibald Menzies, surgeon and naturalist with the Vancouver Expedition of 1790-95 and one of the first botanists to collect plants from the Pacific Northwest. The specific name means rusty and refers to the rusty-colored glands that cover the plant.

PINK MOUNTAIN-HEATHER   *Phyllodoce empetriformis*
A dwarf evergreen shrub with short, numerous, linear, needle-like leaves. The shrub seldom exceeds 20 inches tall. The conspicuous flowers are deep pink or rose, urn-shaped and clustered in umbels. HABITAT/RANGE: An inhabitant of moist to wet soils or open rocky slopes, forests, and higher alpine elevations. It is widely distributed from Alaska to Alberta, south to Colorado and Central California. Blooms from late June to early August. FACTS/USES: The Greek generic name, *Phyllodoce*, is that of a sea nymph. The specific name means empetrum-leaved. Heathers and heaths are attractive ornamental shrubs. Scottish heaths are a close relative to our native species. But our native species is difficult to transplant, and it is nearly impossible to produce flowers on a transplanted shrub.

WOODLAND PINEDROPS   *Pterospora andromedea*

This plant is a saprophyte. Lacking chlorophyll, it derives its food from dead and decaying plant material. The tall, reddish-brown, hairy-glandular stems, up to three feet tall, lack leaves and green color. The yellow, bell-like pendulous flowers are arranged in a widely spaced raceme. The whole plant turns rusty-brown at maturity and persists as a dried stalk through the winter. HABITAT/RANGE: It is very dependent upon the deep humus of coniferous forests, often found under lodge-pole or ponderosa pines. Distributed from Alaska to Alberta and south to Mexico and California. Blooms from late June into August. FACTS/USES: The generic name is derived from the Greek *pteron*, meaning wing, and *sporos*, meaning seed. The seeds of this species have a netlike wing on one end.

PINK PYROLA   *Pyrola asarifolia*

Pink pyrola is a small, perennial, woodland herb with slender, creeping rhizomes. A stem eight to 16 inches high arises form a basal rosette of shiny green, round or kidney-shaped leaves. The pink to purplish five-petaled flowers are waxy in appearance and hang down in racemes. The style extends beyond the open petals and curves outward, giving the appearance of an elephant's trunk. HABITAT/RANGE: Pink pyrola inhabits moist soils, especially in shaded woods near springs. Widely distributed across North America from Alaska to Newfoundland and south to New York, Minnesota, New Mexico and California. Blooms from late June to early August. FACTS/USES: The Latin generic name, *pyrola*, means pear, because the leaves of some species are somewhat pear-shaped. The specific name, *asarifolia*, means asarum-leaved.

ONE-SIDED WINTERGREEN   *Pyrola secunda*

These small, coniferous forest-dwelling flowers ascend two to eight inches from branching, slender rootstocks and com-monly form dense colonies. The small, bell-shaped, green-ish-white flowers are borne in a short, one-sided raceme, which usually bends gracefully downward. Each flower has a long style with a knob-like stigma that projects beyond the corolla. The leaves are a half inch to two and a half inches long, and are ovate, with minutely scalloped edges. HABI-TAT/RANGE: One-sided wintergreen is a dweller of moist, coniferous woods from Alaska to Newfoundland and the Atlantic Coast, south to Mexico and southern California. Flowering period: June-August. FACTS/USES: One-sided Wintergreen's leaves are olive-green and retain their color throughout winter, as suggested by their common name.

BIG HUCKLEBERRY   *Vaccinium membranaceum*

Big huckleberry is a fairly large shrub ranging from two to four feet in height. The woody stems are erect and greatly branched with younger, somewhat angled greenish twigs bearing the elliptic, finely serrated leaves. The small, inconspicuous, greenish to pink, translucent, pendulous, urn-shaped flowers are hidden below the leaves. The fruit is a flattened-globe-shaped berry, which ranges from wine-colored to nearly black. HABITAT/RANGE: This species prefers northern expoouroo of dry or moist sites, sandy or gravelly loams and often can be the dominant understory of coniferous montane forests. It typically occurs from Alaska to Michigan and south to Wyoming, Idaho and northern California. Flowers mid-May to July, with fruits usually appearing in early August. FACTS/USES: The berries are an important food for wildlife, especially bears, and for humans.

GROUSE WHORTLEBERRY   *Vaccinium scoparium*

The stems of this dwarf shrub, which usually grow between four and eight inches high, are its distinguishing characteristic. The green angular branches have the appearance of twisted wrought iron and form a thick, broom-like thatch. Thin, bright green, elliptic, finely serrated margined leaves alternate along the branches. Small, inconspicuous, waxy, pale pink, urn-shaped flowers hang from the leaf axils. These mature into small, edible, bright red berries. HABITAT/RANGE: A timberline species of moist subalpine to alpine woods and open slopes, grouse whortleberry is found from British Columbia to Alberta, south to New Mexico and California. Flowers during June and July, with berries maturing by late July. FACTS/USES: The specific name means broom-like. The berries are an important food for small mammals and birds. They are tart but flavorful and generally are not consumed by humans because of their small size.

Primrose Family
Primulaceae

DARK-THROAT SHOOTING STAR   *Dodecatheon pulchellum*

Shooting stars bear clusters of bright pink flowers with reflexed petals, exposing a yellow stamen tube that forms a downward pointing beak. The flowers are borne on slender, leafless stalks, six to 12 inches above a basal rosette of erect, broadly oblanceolate leaves. As the brown seed capsules mature, they assume an upright position. HABITAT/RANGE: This species widely inhabits coastal prairies and saline swamps, stream banks and wet to moist mountain meadows from sea level to above timberline. It is distributed from Alaska to Pennsylvania to Mexico. Blooms between April and August, depending on elevation and latitude. FACTS/USES: The generic name is derived from the Greek words *dodeka*, for 12, and *theos*, for god, meaning the 12 gods, or the plant protected by the Greek gods. The specific name means pretty or beautiful, referring to the flaring, colorful flower.

ROCKY MOUNTAIN DOUGLASIA　　*Douglasia montana*

Douglasia is a low, spreading, perennial cushion plant formed of a mass of compacted leaves and branches. The leaves are linear-lanceolate and minutely serrate. Short single flower stems—one to three inches tall—arise from the mat of leaves. Each flower is bright pink to rose-violet and possesses a funnel-shaped corolla tube with five flaring lobes. The stamens are attached inside the corolla tube, opposite the petals, and never project above the tube. These distinguishing characteristics help differentiate this species from moss campion (Silene acaulis), which has 10 stamens. HABITAT/RANGE: Prefers dry, open, windswept ridges and scree slopes from the foothills to mountain tops. It is narrowly distributed, primarily in the Central Rockies of southern British Columbia, Montana, Wyoming and Idaho. Flowers from early spring to July. FACTS/USES: The generic name honors David Douglas, 1789-1834, a Northwest botanist and explorer.

PARRY'S PRIMROSE　　*Primula parryi*

Bright reddish-purple flowers with a yellow eye and occurrence at high elevations distinguish this wildflower. The fleshy, leafless stems rise three to 16 inches from a basal rosette of long, smooth, thick, oblong leaves. The bell-shaped flowers have five round lobes and are borne in an umbel of three to 12 flowers. This species is one of the largest wildflowers of the alpine zone. HABITAT/RANGE: Parry's primrose typically occurs on wet sites in subalpine or alpine rock crevices, on talus slopes or in meadows. Its distribution is limited to the Central Rockies, including Idaho and Montana, south to New Mexico and Arizona. Flowers generally during midsummer. FACTS/USES: The common and specific names honor Charles C. Parry, a 19th century English botanist and geologist. The flowers produce an ill-smelling odor, which may attract flies, the primary pollinators of alpine regions.

Gentian Family
Gentianceae

GREEN GENTIAN　　*Frasera speciosa*

Green gentian is a tall, robust biennial that produces a rosette of large, pale green, oblong or spatulate leaves its first summer. In its second summer, it becomes a stout one- to seven-foot stem bearing whorls of lance-shaped leaves that progressively become smaller toward the top. Nestled among the upper whorls of leaves are numerous greenish-white flowers, nearly an inch wide. Each flower has a four-lobed corolla, each lobe flecked with purple dots, and two oval nectary glands fringed with pink hairs. HABITAT/RANGE: This conspicuous species grows on open or wooded foothills and in valleys to subalpine altitudes. It is distributed from Washington to the Dakotas, south to New Mexico, Mexico and California. Flowers during June, July and early August. FACTS/USES: The generic name honors John Fraser (1750-1811), an English nurseryman. The specific name means very showy. The fleshy taproots are edible raw, roasted or boiled.

MOUNTAIN GENTIAN   *Gentiana calycosa*

Mountain gentian is a low, erect, perennial herb that attains a height of four to 12 inches above a fleshy root. This species grows in a tuft and generally produces a solitary flower on each stem. The bell-shaped corolla is dark blue with a greenish interior. Each flower has five rounded lobes with pleats in between. Each pleat usually terminates with two fine, pointed teeth. The ovate leaves are opposite and the lower leaves are joined, forming a sheath around the stem. HABITAT/RANGE. Mountain gentian prefers wet meadows, stream banks or open slopes in subalpine or alpine zones. It is a widely distributed cordilleran species of British Columbia and Alberta, south to Utah and central California. Flowers from July to September. FACTS/USES: The generic name is for King Gentius of Illyria, an ancient country of southern Europe on the Adriatic; Gentius knew of medicinal uses for the herb. The specific name means calyx-like.

WESTERN FRINGED GENTIAN   *Gentiana detonsa*

The flowers of this annual species are an elegant bluish purple with a one- to two-inch-long, bell-shaped corolla topped with four fringed petals, which twist together and close in dim light. Several stems may arise four to 16 inches from a branched base. The two to four pairs of opposite, narrow lanceolate leaves are found basally and along the stem. HABITAT/RANGE: This dweller of wet soils and bogs is found along streams and in meadows from mid elevations to the subalpine zone. It is a circumboreal species and is found from Alaska to Newfoundland, south to New York, Indiana, South Dakota, Mexico and California. Flowers from late June to late August. FACTS/USES: The specific name means clipped, referring to the fringed petals. Gentian roots have been used medicinally as a mild gastric stimulant to aid digestion. In 1926, it was chosen the official flower of Yellowstone National Park because of its association with thermal basins.

Milkweed Family
Asclepiadaceae

SHOWY MILKWEED   *Asclepias speciosa*

The foliage of this erect, stout perennial attains a height of one to five feet and is entirely covered with short, satiny, grayish hairs. When the foliage is broken, it produces a thick, milky juice. The flowers are arranged in umbels that are borne on stalks from the axils of the upper leaves. The leaves are large, opposite, ovate or broadly lanceolate. Each small flower is comprised of five reddish, recurved sepals, five pinkish or purplish petals and five hornlike hoods, which curve inward. The fruit is a large, three-inch-long, plump pod, which, upon opening, produces a brown flat seed with a silky tuft of hair. HABITAT/RANGE: It commonly is found on dry-to-moist sandy or loamy soils along watercourses or in disturbed sites of the montane zone. Well-distributed from British Columbia to the central United States and California. Blooms from June to August. FACTS/USES: This species is edible, but some species of milkweeds are poisonous.

Morning Glory
Family
Convolvulaceae

BINDWEED   *Convolvulus arvensis*

Bindweed has white or pinkish funnel-shaped flowers, nearly an inch wide. One or two flowers usually arise per leaf axil along a prostrate trailing or climbing stem one to four feet long. The perennial root system is extensive and forms a dense tangled mat. The leaves are spaced alternately along the stem and are triangular or arrow- or ovate-shaped, usually with sharp-pointed lobes. The fruit is a small, globose capsule, usually containing four dull brown seeds. HABITAT/RANGE: Bindweed was introduced from Europe and has invaded and adapted to moist sites in farm fields, along roadsides and in other disturbed areas of low to mid elevations. Found throughout North America, except extreme southern and northern regions. Blooms May to October. FACTS/USES: The generic name means to twine, and the specific name means pertaining to cultivated fields. Because of its habitual adaptation and extensive root system, it is difficult to eradicate.

Dogbane Family
Apocynaceae

SPREADING DOGBANE   *Apocynum androsaemifolium*

Dogbane is an erect, perennial, bushy herb that rises eight to 20 inches from tough, woody rhizomes. The herbage, when broken, produces a bitter, milky, rubber-containing juice, distasteful and poisonous to domestic stock. The forked stems bear drooping, opposite, ovate or oblong leaves and clusters or cymes of small white or pink flowers at the ends of branches. Each quarter-inch flower is bell-shaped, with a five-lobed corolla. The slender seed pods, up to five inches long, split along one side and disperse numerous seeds, each with a tuft of silky hairs at one end. HABITAT/RANGE: Frequently found on dry hillsides in coniferous forests and often forms dense stands on overused areas from the foothills to the subalpine zone. Found throughout North America, except extreme southern and northern regions. Flowers from June to September. FACTS/USES: The Greek generic name is derived from *apo*, away from, and *kynos*, for dog.

Phlox Family
Polemoniaceae

COLLOMIA   *Collomia linearis*

Collomia is a small, spindly, single-stemmed, usually un-branched annual herb only three to 10 inches high. The tiny quarter-inch-long pink or lavender tubular corollas are borne in dense terminal clusters interspersed with leafy bracts. The leaves are long, narrow and tapered. HABITAT/RANGE: This plant is found on dry-to-moist soils, especially on disturbed sites along horse trails and roads from lowlands to high-mountain elevations. This is a widespread native plant of western North America. Flowers from early spring to midsummer, depending upon available moisture. FACTS/USES: The generic name, *Collomia*, is derived from the Greek work *kolla*, which means glue, referring to the seeds. The seeds of this species produce a mucus coating when they become moist. The specific name, *linearis*, means linear and refers to the leaf shape.

SCARLET GILIA   *Gilia aggregata*

This plant is a showy biennial that produces a rosette of pinnately divided leaves its first year and a one- to three-foot flowering stalk the second year. Bright red trumpet-shaped corollas are one to two inches long with five or more backward-flaring lobes. The flowers are arranged in clusters. The leaves are finely, pinnately divided into fingerlike segments. HABITAT/RANGE: A common Western wildflower preferring well-drained soils in open meadows or lightly wooded sites, as well as sagebrush valleys and mountain ridges. Widely distributed from British Columbia to Alberta, south to Texas, northern Mexico and California. Blooms from May through July. FACTS/USES: The specific name means aggregate or clustered. Dense patches often are found among sagebrush. Blooming around the fourth of July, they form a brilliant red display.

HOOD'S PHLOX   *Phlox hoodii*

A very low, mat-forming perennial with taproots and woody bases, branching into trailing stems. The opposite, narrow, linear leaves are prickly and somewhat wooly. The five-petaled corollas are white but fade to pink or lilac at maturity. HABITAT/RANGE: A widespread plant found in open forests, on windswept, gravelly ridges up to timberline, but more commonly in drier sites in sagebrush foothills, valleys and plains. In lower elevations, this plant is an early spring bloomer; it blooms into midsummer at higher elevations. FACTS/USES: This wildflower forms dense carpet-like mats covered with white-petaled flowers. At lower elevations, the plants are loose and sprawling with stems that reach six inches high. At higher elevations, especially on open windswept ridges, the plants become compact, tufted mats with flowers barely projecting above the mat.

LONG-LEAF PHLOX   *Phlox longifolia*

Long-leaf phlox is a taller plant than the mat-forming phloxes. It stands four to 15 inches high and grows in dense, loose-spreading clumps. The leaves are slender, opposite, pointed and one to three inches long. The half-inch-long corolla tube has five lobes and ranges in color from white, as it first emerges, to pink or light blue as it ages. HABITAT/RANGE: Often associated with sagebrush and well-drained, rocky soils from the lowlands to mid- or, occasionally, high-mountain elevations. It is a widespread flower throughout the West, from British Columbia and Montana south to New Mexico and southern California. Flowers late spring into early summer. FACTS/USES: The specific name means long-leaved. The Greek generic name, *phlox*, means flame and refers to the brightly colored flowers. This species has become a favorite in cultivated gardens.

SHOWY POLEMONIUM   *Polemonium pulcherrimum*
Flowers are a sky-blue color with five yellow stamens that do not extend beyond the corolla. The corolla has five lobes, which spread outward. This perennial herb ascends from a woody, extensive rootstock with the stems somewhat trailing or lax. Most of the leaves are basal and pinnately divided into paired leaflets, giving the leaves a ladder-like appearance, hence another common name, Jacob's ladder. This species is less glandular and odoriferous than *P. viscosum*. HABITAT/ RANGE: Often found on moist-to-dry, gravelly or rocky soils from mid to high elevations. It often is associated with lodge-pole pine or spruce-fir stands. Occurs from Washington to Montana, south to Colorado and Nevada. Flowers from June to July. FACTS/USES: The Latin specific name means very handsome. The generic name probably is from the Greek philosopher Polemon.

SKUNK POLEMONIUM   *Polemonium viscosum*
This plant has bright and showy purple, funnel-shaped, five-lobed flowers crowded into compact clusters. Orange anthers are highly visible against the flowers. The leafy stems reach four to 16 inches high and grow in dense clumps. Each long, narrow leaf is pinnately divided into 30 to 40 whorled, ovate leaflets. Sticky, glandular hairs cover the stems and leaves and emit a skunk-like scent. HABITAT/RANGE: This plant prefers high mountains and even tundra on open, rocky ridges and disturbed sites such as road cuts and pocket-gopher trenches. Distributed from Washington to Alberta, south to New Mexico and central Nevada. Blooms June to August. FACTS/USES: The specific name, *viscosum*, means sticky. The skunk-like smell produced by the sticky glands may be a defense against or a distractant to grazing animals.

Waterleaf Family
Hydrophyllaceae

BALLHEAD WATERLEAF   *Hydrophyllum capitatum*
Ballhead waterleaf is a low-growing, perennial plant, four to 15 inches tall. The floral heads bloom below, and sometimes are hidden by, the leaves. The lavender, ball-like heads—hence the common and specific names—are comprised of numerous, densely congested, cup-shaped, five-petaled flowers with five stamens and two-lobed stigma projecting beyond the corolla, giving the heads a bristly appearance. The pinnately compound, deeply lobed leaves have long, succulent petioles, usually attached below the ground. HABITAT/RANGE: This herb has a wide range of habitats from dry plains to subalpine mountain ridges but prefers the montane zone, especially along the break between aspen groves and sagebrush. Found from southern British Columbia and Alberta to Colorado and central California. One of the first spring and early summer flowers. FACTS/USES: The generic name is derived from the Greek words *hydro*, for water, and *phyllon*, for leaf.

SILVERLEAF PHACELIA   *Phacelia hastata*

Silverleaf phacelia grows from a stout rootstock six to 15 inches tall, with lax and spreading stems. The leaves are distinctive, lanceolate, prominently veined and densely covered with grayish hairs that lie flat. Clustered along the stem are dense flowering heads of white to pale purple flowers. Each flower is comprised of a funnel-shaped corolla, five-lobed and with five stamens that protrude beyond the petals, giving the flower heads a bristly appearance. HABITAT/RANGE: Silverleaf phacella prefers dry, open sltes, especially in association with sagebrush, from plains to timberline. Phacelia is well-distributed throughout the West, from southern British Columbia and Alberta to New Mexico. Usually flowers between May and July. FACTS/USES: The generic name was derived from the Greek word *phakelos*, for fascicle, in reference to the bundled flower heads. Some phacelia species are edible, primarily as cooked greens.

SILKY PHACELIA   *Phacelia sericea*

Brilliant purple flowers arranged in dense, bottle-brush-like spikes distinguish this flower of the high mountains. Individual flowers are comprised of five round petals fused at the base, forming a saucer-shaped corolla, and five purple stamens tipped with yellow anthers extending outward. Several stems usually form a clump and grow five to 16 inches tall from the crown of a branching taproot. The broad lanceolate leaves have narrow, irregular pinnately cleft lobes and are densely covered with grayish, silky hairs. HABITAT/RANGE: Silky phacelia is a common wildflower of open, rocky or gravelly hillsides or mountain ridges, especially disturbed soils, ranging from the montane to alpine zones. This is a well-distributed cordilleran species of southern to western Canada and the western states, except Oregon. Flowers June to August, depending on latitude. FACTS/USES: The specific name means silky, referring to the silky pubescence of the leaves.

Borage Family
Boraginaceae

BRISTLY CRYPTANTHA   *Cryptantha interrupta*

Bristly cryptantha is a perennial forb four to 20 inches in height. It ascends from a taproot and has a woody caudex from which a tuft of basal, oblanceolate leaves grow, often with remnants of previous years' leaves on the bottom. The entire plant is covered with coarse hairs or bristles and, with the aid of a hand lens, minute blisters can be seen at the base of the bristles on the lower leaves. Each small, white flower is congested in the inflorescence and has petals that are fused into a tube with five spreading lobes. The fruit is a nutlet. HABITAT/RANGE: This species prefers dry, sandy or clay soils of sagebrush plains or exposed ridges at low to high elevations. It is fairly rare and has a limited distribution from Washington to Montana, south to Wyoming and Nevada. Blooms in early summer. FACTS/USES: This plant belongs to a large genus, and species differentiation can be difficult.

HOUND'S TONGUE   *Cynoglossum officinale*

This biennial species produces a rosette of oblong- to lance-shaped, velvety-white leaves with a tonguelike venation pattern—hence the common name—its first year. The second year, a one- to four-foot flowering stalk emerges. The small quarter-inch-wide, reddish-purple flowers are borne in several loose racemes at the end of the stem. Each flower matures into four prickly nutlets, which spread by attaching to the coats of passing animals. HABITAT/RANGE: Frequently found on dry, sandy, disturbed sites, especially along roadsides, near buildings and in overused pastures. It was introduced from Europe and has become well-established throughout temperate North America. Flowers during summer. FACTS/USES: The Greek generic name is derived from *kynos*, for dog, and *glossa*, for tongue, referring to the tonguelike appearance and roughness of the leaves of some species. Contains carcinogenic alkoloids but is used medincinally.

ALPINE FORGET-ME-NOT   *Eritrichium nanum*

Alpine forget-me-not is a long-lived, small—seldom more than four inches high—tightly matted, cushion plant. The minute, compact leaves are sparsely covered with long hairs, visible with a hand magnifying lens. Rising just above the mat are small (quarter-inch in diameter) dark blue, or occasionally white, yellow-eyed funnel-shaped flowers with five round lobes. A related species *(E. howardii)* is densely covered with coarse silvery-stringose hairs. HABITAT/RANGE: This species has adapted to withstand the harsh winds of exposed rocky ridges and mountain crests from the subalpine to the arctic zones. It has circumboreal distribution, but in the Rocky Mountain Region is found along mountain ranges from Alaska south to New Mexico. Blooms during July and August. FACTS/USES: The generic name is derived from the Greek words *erion*, for wool, and *trichos*, for hair, and refers to the wooly pubescence. The specific name means dwarf.

MANY-FLOWERED STICKSEED   *Hackelia floribunda*

Many-flowered stickseed is a leafy, erect, tall (to three feet) biennial or short-lived perennial herb. The hairy leaves are long and lanceolate with petioles and become progressively smaller and stalkless toward the top of the plant. Near the top in loose, branched clusters, are small, quarter-inch-diameter, pale blue flowers. Each flower is funnel-shaped with five flaring lobes and a yellow center. The pistil matures into four small nutlets, each with several rows of barbed prickles, which adhere to the coats of passing animals. HABITAT/RANGE: Prefers moist meadows, woodlands and thickets from the foothills to mid-mountain elevations. It is distributed from British Columbia to Saskatchewan, south to New Mexico and California. Flowers between June and August. FACTS/USES: The generic name honors Joseph Hackel (1783-1869), a Czechoslovakian botanist. The specific name means free-flowering, in reference to its numerous flowers.

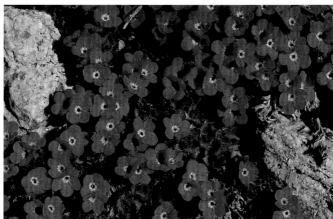

WESTERN STICKSEED — *Lappula redowskii*

This taprooted annual is an erect herb, weedy in appearance, and grows six to 18 inches tall. The flowers are borne in a tight bracteate, false raceme. Each white to pale blue flower is less than a quarter-inch in diameter, cuplike, with five lobes and relatively inconspicuous. The foliage and stems are hairy and the leaves are linear. Flowers mature into a nutlet with a single row of marginal prickles, which cling to passing animals. This species is very similar to many-flowered stickseed (*Hackelia floribunda*). The main differences of this species are: it has smaller flowers; it is an annual; and it has the single row of barbed prickles on the nutlet. HABITAT/RANGE: Western stickseed grows around buildings and along trails and roadsides, especially on disturbed sites, from low- to mid-mountain elevations of the Rocky Mountain states. Blooms June to August. FACTS/USES: The Latin generic name is from *lappa*, meaning a little bur.

STONESEED — *Lithospermum ruderale*

Several leafy stems—one to two feet tall—arise from a strong, woody taproot and form a large clump, with the dried remnant of last year's stems often projecting from the base. Long, narrow, sharply pointed, lanceolate leaves clasp the stem. Both stems and leaves are covered with long white hairs. Among the axils of the upper leaves are clusters of small, pale yellow, five-lobed, funnel-shaped flowers. Each flower produces four shiny, hard, gray nutlets nearly a quarter-inch long. HABITAT/RANGE: Prefers open, dry sites on slopes and in grasslands, often in association with sagebrush and juniper, at low to mid elevations. It is common in western Canada, south to Colorado and northern California. Blooms during early summer. FACTS/USES: The specific name is derived from the Greek words *lithos*, for stone, and *sperma*, for seed, in reference to the hard seeds. Native Americans used this plant for birth control. The roots also were used for red dye.

MOUNTAIN BLUEBELL — *Mertensia ciliata*

Mountain bluebell is a tall, leafy perennial herb. The stems usually are clustered and attain heights of up to five feet. The leaves are somewhat hairy, blister-dotted, egg-shaped and ciliate or hairy-fringed along the margin. Clusters of blue, tubular-shaped flowers hang loosely from the nodding stems. As the flowers mature, they turn pink and a threadlike stalk or style protrudes from the blossom and is persistent after the nutlet ripens. HABITAT/RANGE: This species prefers moist sites of rich loam soils, especially along streams and seeps from low to alpine elevations. Distributed from central Oregon to Montana, south to Colorado, Nevada and California. Flowers from early to mid-August, depending on elevation. FACTS/USES: The Latin specific name is derived from the word *cilium*, for eyelid, and refers to the ciliate hairs on the leaf margin.

MOUNTAIN FORGET-ME-NOT   *Myosotis sylvatica*

This perennial herb usually grows in a clump of one to several stems, four to 12 inches tall. The tufted basal leaves are lanceolate to oblong in shape, with the upper stem leaves smaller in size and sessile. Both stems and leaves are covered with long, soft hairs. The flared, disk-shaped flowers are brilliant, deep blue with five round lobes and yellow to pink centers. Hidden within the corolla tube are five stamens. The small flowers, only a quarter-inch in diameter, are fragrant. Four shiny, black seeds develop per flower and are enclosed within the hairy sepals. HABITAT/RANGE: Mountain forget-me-not is a circumboreal species that inhabits meadows and moist sites from the montane to the alpine zones, from Alaska to Colorado, Utah and Oregon. Blooms during summer. FACTS/USES: The generic name is derived form the Greek words *mus*, for mouse, and *ous*, for ear, referring to the hairiness of the foliage. This is the state flower of Alaska.

Mint Family
Lamiaceae

GIANT-HYSSOP   *Agastache urticifolia*

A robust perennial herb with four-sided stems, reaching one to five feet in height, and opposite, ovate, toothed leaves, which usually are smooth on the upper surface and lighter colored beneath. The white to purplish flowers are clustered on a dense terminal spike. The corolla has two pairs of stamens, which extend beyond the lobes, with the upper pair longer than the lower pair. HABITAT/RANGE: It prefers moist soils of riparian habitats to open hillsides from the foothills to lower subalpine regions. Ranges from southeast British Columbia to Montana and south to Colorado and California. Blooms from mid-June to mid-August. FACTS/USES: The generic name is derived from the Greek, *agan*, meaning much, and *stachys*, meaning ear of grain, and referring to the inflorescence. The nutlet-like seeds may be eaten raw or cooked.

FIELD MINT   *Mentha arvensis*

Field mint is an aromatic perennial with opposite leaves, four-angled stems and numerous small rose-pink flowers densely clustered in axillary whorls. The leaves are broadly lanceolate with sharp-toothed margins. The plant rises one to three feet from long, horizontal, creeping rootstocks. HABITAT/RANGE: This species commonly occurs in wet or moist soils along streams, springs and seeps, and often grows among shrubs. It is a circumboreal species and ranges in North America from British Columbia to Saskatchewan, south to Nebraska, New Mexico and California. Blooms during late summer from July to September. FACTS/USES: The specific name means pertaining to cultivated fields. The generic name is derived from the Greek name *Minthe*, a nymph who was fabled to have been changed into a mint plant by Proserpine. The dried or fresh leaves of this plant make an excellent tea.

HORSEMINT
Monarda fistulosa

Horsemint is a showy, aromatic perennial with opposite, toothed, ovate leaves. The stems are four-angled and one to two feet tall, ending in a dense terminal head of purple flowers. Each individual flower is a two-lipped corolla. The upper lip bears two stamens, which protrude outward, and the lower lip is three-lobed. HABITAT/RANGE: Grows in moist to dry soils of meadows, ravines and roadsides from low to mid elevations in the mountains. Found along the Rocky Mountains and east to Manitoba and Texas. Blooms from mid-June to early August. FACTS/USES: The generic name, *monarda*, is derived from the name of an early Spanish physician and botanist, Monardes. The specific name means hollow and cylindrical. Horsemint can be used for tea, but it does not make a highly palatable drink, and a strong brew can cause stomach distress.

SELF-HEAL
Prunella vulgaris

This low perennial herb ascends four to eight inches from a branching rootstock. It is a typical member of the mint family, possessing a square stem, opposite leaves and two-lipped flowers. The irregular flowers have graceful hoods, which form an upper lip and a three-lobed lower lip, the broader middle lobe bearing a fringe along the margin. The purple flowers are arranged in a short, leafy, densely clustered, terminal spike. HABITAT/RANGE: Grows on moist soils of open meadows and shaded woods from sea level to the montane zones. It is a widely distributed circumboreal species of cool and temperate climates. Blooms during summer. FACTS/USES: The specific name means common. As the common name suggests, this plant has been an important medicinal plant. The ground leaves or roots, used in tea, have been used to treat sore throats, fevers, diarrhea, wounds, sores and stomach cramps. The active compound is ursolic acid.

MARSH SKULLCAP
Scutellaria galericulata

Marsh skullcap is a perennial herb with erect, one- to three-foot, slender, square stems, which rise from creeping underground rootstocks. The lance-shaped, opposite leaves bear a single flower from each of the upper leaf axils. Each blue to purplish flower is tubular-shaped and bilabiate. The upper lip is helmet-shaped and the lower is bent downward. HABITAT/ RANGE: Skullcap inhabits wet or boggy ground and often shallow water, around meadows, lakes, ponds and ditches, from the foothills to the montane zones. This species is widespread and circumboreal and is found from Alaska to northern New Mexico and central California. Flowers from June to September. FACTS/USES: The specific name means helmetlike and refers to the upper lip of the corolla. Other members of the genus are used medicinally in a mild tea as a tonic, antispasmodic and stringent. The active agent is scutellarin, a flavonoid compound.

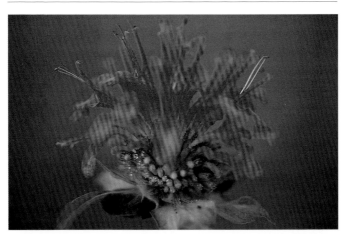

Potato Family
Solanaceae

HENBANE   *Hyoscyamus niger*

This coarse, strong-scented, sticky plant is an annual or biennial that grows one to three feet tall. The stalkless leaves are pubescent, lanceolate or ovate in outline, coarsely toothed and shallowly lobed. The greenish or brownish-yellow flowers with dark purple veins and centers are borne terminally or in leaf axils. As the plant matures, the terminal growth produces new flowers while older flowers, down the stem, are bearing fruit. The fruit is a dry, urn-shaped seed capsule, which contains numerous poppy-like seeds. HABITAT/RANGE: Henbane commonly occurs along roadsides and other waste areas from the lowlands into the mountains. It is an introduced species from Europe and has become established throughout most of the United States. Blooms late May to July. FACTS/USES: The generic name is derived from the Greek word, *hyoskyamos*, meaning sow bean. The specific name means black. It is a poisonous plant containing atropine.

GROUNDCHERRY   *Physalis longifolia*

This well-branched perennial herb ascends eight to 25 inches from a running rhizome, and often forms clumps. The alternate leaves are ovate to ovate-oblong and entire to shallowly toothed. Pale yellow, bell-shaped flowers with purple centers hang pendulously from the terminals or from leaf axils. The calyx enlarges to yellow or brown, five- to 10-angled, paper-like lantern, which encloses a small tomato-like fruit. HABITAT/RANGE: Groundcherry commonly grows on moist to medium-dry soils along roadsides, in wastelands, or cultivated fields, and other disturbed sites. It is a native plant but found primarily on the east slope of the Cascade Mountains into the Great Plains. Flowers during June and July. FACTS/USES: The generic name is derived from the Greek word for bladder and refers to the inflated calyx. The specific name means long-leaved. The fruit is potentially toxic but can be eaten raw like tomatoes.

CLIMBING NIGHTSHADE   *Solanum dulcamara*

Climbing nightshade rises one to nine feet from a perennial, rhizomatous, woody root. The recumbent stems climb or scramble among shrubs or on fences for support and bear ovate-cordate leaves with a prominent pair of basal lobes. Near the end of branches are purple, starlike flowers with five reflexed petals and five yellow stamens, which form a projecting cone. The fruit matures into a bright red, shiny berry with numerous seeds. HABITAT/RANGE: This native of Eurasia is well-established in North America, especially in disturbed areas in thickets, clearings and open woods. It grows from sea level to the montane zone, but is infrequent in arid regions. It has a long flowering season—May until the first frosts. FACTS/USES: Most members of the nightshade family are toxic, and this species is not an exception. It contains steroids, alkaloids and glucosides, which cause vomiting, vertigo and paralysis, but in proper dosage, it can be used medicinally.

WYOMING PAINTBRUSH — *Castilleja linariaefolia*

Wyoming paintbrush is a bright red, showy plant, but the red portion is not the flower. The flower itself is tubular and yellow-green in color, and not particularly attractive. Surrounding the flower is a brightly colored leaflike bract. The leaves are long, linear and cut into slender segments near the top. The botanical differences between the numerous paintbrush species often are minute and distinguishing them may be difficult. HABITAT/RANGE: Inhabits dry to moist sagebrush slopes and juniper woodlands. Distributed from Oregon to Montana, south to New Mexico and southern California. Blooms June through July. FACTS/USES: The specific name, *linariaefolia*, means linaria-leaved, referring to the toadflax-like leaf. In 1917, the Wyoming Legislature selected this species as the state flower.

COMMON PAINTBRUSH — *Castilleja miniata*

Paintbrush is perhaps one of the most recognizable and common plants of the West. The stems of this species often form large clumps that reach one to two feet tall. The greenish-red tipped corollas do not extend conspicuously beyond the colorful red, leafy bracts. The leaves are long and linear, and the upper leaves and colorful bracts may have three lobes. HABITAT/RANGE: A dweller of south-facing, well-drained slopes of mid-elevations. Distributed from Alaska to Alberta, south to New Mexico and southern California, missing the Oregon and Washington coast ranges. A late spring and summer bloomer. FACTS/USES: Most paintbrushes are semiparasitic, producing some of their own food and deriving water and nutrients from the roots of a host plant, usually sagebrush. This system allows them to adapt to drier conditions.

SULFUR PAINTBRUSH — *Castilleja sulphurea*

The stems arise singly or in small clumps from a short ascending rootstock. The inflorescence is a dense spike with pale to bright yellow ovate bracts, which are mistaken for the flowers. But the flowers appear above the bracts as a long tubular corolla projecting from an outer tubelike sheath called a calyx. HABITAT/RANGE: Prefers moist to dry soils of meadows, plains, foothills and rocky slopes into the higher mountains. A strictly Rocky Mountain species, from southern Alberta to New Mexico. Blooms late May through July. FACTS/USES: A special delight for young Indian children was to pull the tubular flowers and suck out their sweet nectar. Most paintbrush species have a wide variation in color. Sulfur paintbrush, however, is one of the few species that is yellow with little variation.

BLUE-EYED MARY
Collinsia parviflora

This is a small, delicate annual with slender, widely branched stems. The narrow, lanceolate purple-tinged leaves are opposite, or sometimes whorled in the flower axils. The tiny blue and white flowers are seldom more than a quarter-inch long. The upper lip, bent upward, has two white lobes, while the lower lip has three bright blue lobes (the central lobe is smaller than the lateral ones) projecting forward. HABITAT/RANGE: Blue-eyed Mary inhabits shaded, gravelly flats and disturbed areas where other vegetation is sparse. Found throughout the western states and into southern Canada. Flowers in spring and early summer. FACTS/USES: The generic name, *Collinsia*, is named after an early American botanist, Zacheus Collins. The specific name, *parviflora*, means small-flowered. Blue-eyed Mary is perhaps one of the smallest Western flowers.

DALMATIAN TOADFLAX
Linaria dalmatica

This large robust perennial herb grows two to four feet high. The stem—woody at the base—and leaves are grayish-green and glaucous. The opposite leaves are stiff, broad, ovate and clasp the stem. Flowers are arranged in terminal elongate racemes. They are bright yellow, but often purplish tinged at the apex. Corollas are one to two inches, two-lipped and lobed. The lower lip has formed an orange palate at the entrance of the throat. HABITAT/RANGE: A native of the Mediterranean region, Dalmatian toadflax has established itself in scattered regions throughout North America and is spreading. It prefers disturbed areas along roads, near dwellings and sagebrush flats. Blooms July through September. FACTS/USES: Toadflax is very similar to its close relation, butter and eggs. The difference is that toadflax is larger with broader leaves that clasp the stem.

BUTTER AND EGGS
Linaria vulgaris

This showy perennial herb ascends one to three feet from creeping rhizomes and often grows in patches displaying brilliant yellow flowers. Each flower, tipped upward and arranged in a dense raceme, has a yellow corolla with an upper two-lobed lip and a lower lip raised into an orange palate. An awl-shaped spur projects below the corolla. The stems bear simple, sessile, linear, pale-green leaves. HABITAT/RANGE: An introduced weedy species from Eurasia, butter and eggs has become established in disturbed pastures and roadsides throughout temperate North America. A summer bloomer. FACTS/USES: The common name is taken from the flowers' color combination, and the Latin genus name is derived from *linum*, the genus of flax, because the leaves resemble this species. It is believed that a tea made from this plant is good for skin eruptions, jaundice and as a laxative.

YELLOW MONKEY-FLOWER   *Mimulus guttatus*

This showy perennial has bright yellow, tubular corollas, which are two-lipped and five-lobed, with two ridges extending back from the lower lip into the throat. The throat is spotted with red, and the flowers are one to two inches long. The hollow, square stems bear opposite, lance-shaped leaves and flowers, usually in pairs from the axils of the upper leaves. This species is quite variable in form and size, ranging from a few inches to several feet in height. HABITAT/RANGE: This cordilleran species of North America prefers moist to wet seeps of mountain habitats. An early spring to late fall bloomer, though it can bloom during winter if it is near hot springs. FACTS/USES: The specific name means spotted or speckled. This plant can be eaten raw as a salad additive, though it has a slightly bitter flavor.

LEWIS' MONKEY-FLOWER   *Mimulus lewisii*

Lewis' monkey-flower is a showy, herbaceous perennial with erect stems ascending from rhizomes. The leaves are glabrous to slightly hairy, lance-shaped, and unevenly toothed. The pink-purple, irregular corollas are two-lipped with two lobes above and three lobes below, while the throat has two bright yellow patches. HABITAT/RANGE: This common mountain wildflower grows in dense clumps along moist, wet streams, ravines and seepage areas. Ranges from Alaska south to Utah and California. Blooms late June through August. FACTS/USES: Both the common and specific names pay tribute to Captain Meriwether Lewis, the explorer who first described this plant. The bright rose-pink flowers are attractants for pollination by insects and hummingbirds. As nectary guides entice them into the funnel-shaped throat, anthers, projecting from the roof, dust their backs with pollen.

DWARF PURPLE MONKEY-FLOWER   *Mimulus nanus*

This very small annual grows only a few inches high. The reddish-purple flowers, less than an inch long, appear almost stalkless. The corollas are two-lipped and five-lobed, with yellow and purple marking in the throat. The opposite, lanceolate leaves are covered with glandular hairs, and the flowers are borne in leaf axils near the top of the plant. It can become well-branched and developed on good sites. HABITAT/RANGE: This plant prefers bare, open areas with sliding or loose sandy soil. It also is associated with sagebrush and dry pine forests. Its range is limited to central Washington, south to northern California and as far east as Yellowstone National Park. Blooms early spring and summer, while moisture is available. FACTS/USES: The Latin generic name is derived from *mimus*, meaning mimic, and refers to the grinning pattern of the flower that resembles the masks worn by mimes.

YELLOW OWL-CLOVER   *Orthocarpus luteus*

Yellow owl-clover is an erect, perennial herb that grows singly or in several-stemmed clumps, four to 12 inches high. The plants are glandular-hairy, and the inflorescence is a dense spike of yellow flowers with each beak-like corolla projecting upward. This species is very similar to the louseworts *(Pedicularis)* and to sulfur paintbrush *(Castilleja sulphurea)*. HABITAT/RANGE: An inhabitant of dry, open grasslands, plains and open woods of lowlands to mid-mountain elevations. Occurs from British Columbia, east of the Cascades, to Manitoba, south to Minnesota, Nebraska, Montana, New Mexico and California. Flowers throughout summer. FACTS/USES: The generic name is derived from the Greek words *orthos*, for straight, and *karpos*, for fruit, and refers to the shape of the capsuled fruit. The specific name means yellow.

BRACTED LOUSEWORT   *Pedicularis bracteosa*

A tall, one- to three-foot, perennial herb, this plant has a dense spikelike raceme of pale yellow to maroon or purple-colored flowers. The half-inch-long corolla is two-lipped, with the upper lip arched or hooded (galeate) and the lower lip three-lobed and spread outward. Leaflike bracts project from among the dense flowers (hence the common name). The leaves are long, somewhat fernlike, pinnately compound, with basal leaves larger than stem leaves. HABITAT/RANGE: Prefers moist mountain woods and meadows. This widespread cordilleran species exists from British Columbia, Alberta to Colorado and California. Blooms June to August. FACTS/USES: The Latin genus name, *Pedicularis*, means louse, and relates to the superstition that lice infestations of livestock followed its ingestion. Although this species occasionally is cropped by sheep, it is not considered a valuable forage plant.

WHITE COILED-BEAK   *Pedicularis contorta*

White coiled-beak, as the name implies, possesses a long, downward-coiled petal—actually the upper lip of the corolla tube—which curves like a sickle. The white or cream-colored flowers are arranged in a raceme near the top of a six- to 24-inch stem. The fernlike leaves are pinnately lobed into narrow, sharply toothed segments. Both leaves and stems are maroon-tinged and the alternating stem leaves decrease in size toward the top of the plant. HABITAT/RANGE: White coiled-beak is a widespread plant of mid and upper altitudes, preferring woods and dry, open slopes, but especially subalpine meadows. It is found from Alaska to the Northwest Territories, south to northern Wyoming and northern California. Blooms from June to August. FACTS/USES: The specific name means contorted or twisted. Many species of this group are semiparasitic, deriving nutrients from the roots of other plants.

ELEPHANT'S HEAD   *Pedicularis groenlandica*
This unusual and distinctive purplish flower resembles the head of an elephant. The broad upper lip (galea) of the irregular corolla suggests an elephant's cranium, the prolonged and upward curving beak representing the trunk and the lower corolla lip resembling the ears and lower jaw. The "elephants' heads" are arranged on dense racemes. The long leaves are mostly basal, narrow and pinnately divided, then lobed and toothed, giving them a fernlike appearance. HABITAT/RANGE: This showy, colorful flower usually grows in dense patches of wet or boggy meadows, producing a field of purple. It is distributed widely from Alaska to Labrador and south in the Western states to New Mexico and California. Flowers June to August. FACTS/USES: The specific name, *groenlandica*, means of Greenland, where it first was discovered.

BLUE PENSTEMON   *Penstemon cyaneus*
Blue penstemon is an erect, robust plant (up to three feet tall), with conspicuous blue-violet, bilaterally symmetrical flowers up to two inches long, clustered along the stem. The leathery-like, smooth leaves are narrowly lanceolate or ovate, stalkless and opposite. HABITAT/RANGE: This tall, blue-flowered penstemon is a common species of foothills and typically is found in sandy sagebrush plains and along roadsides, but it has a limited range to eastern Idaho, Montana, Wyoming and northern Colorado and northern Utah. Flowers sometime between May and July. FACTS/USES: *Cyaneus* means blue. The penstemons are some of the Rocky Mountains' most beautiful flowers. Blue penstemon adapts easily to disturbed sites and is a roadside flower frequently found in patches.

HOT ROCK PENSTEMON   *Penstemon deustus*
This plant grows in a dense cluster from a woody base; the previous year's stems and leaves often remain around the base. The leaves are opposite, glabrous, ovate or lanceolate, with sharp teeth along the margin. The two-lipped corolla, one or two inches long, is cream or whitish-colored with purplish guide lines in the throat. HABITAT/RANGE: This plant grows in dry, open rocky sites from lowland to montane areas. It is widespread through the central Rocky Mountains from Washington, to western Montana, south to Utah and central California. An early summer bloomer. FACTS/USES: The specific name means burned. This species is one of the few penstemons with white flowers. Most penstemons are poor seeders and reproduce mainly by rootstocks. On overgrazed ranges, these plants are one of the first to reappear and, if there is an abundance, it is an indication of past overgrazing.

CRESTED TONGUE PENSTEMON *Penstemon eriantherus*
This species is very similar to bush penstemon *(P. fruticosus)*, with the main difference being in the foliage. Crested tongue has stems, five to 15 inches tall, and hairy, glandular leaves. The corollas also are hairy on the outside. The throats of the lilac-lavender corollas have purplish guidelines and usually are prominently yellow-bearded. The plants are ascending and herbaceous. HABITAT/RANGE: This plant has a varied habitat but prefers loose soils of foothills to high plains. It ranges along the Rocky Mountains, from British Columbia to Colorado, and from Oregon to South Dakota. Blooms May through June. FACTS/USES: Most penstemons have little browse value for wildlife or livestock. Sheep do, however, use penstemon—especially at higher elevations where its palatability is considered good.

BUSH PENSTEMON   *Penstemon fruticosus*
Bush penstemon is a sprawling, woody plant, six to 24 inches tall. The lower leaves are opposite, stalkless, spatula-shaped, with or without fine teeth. The upper leaves are shiny, smaller, one-half to one inch long, and egg-shaped. The bright lavender-blue corollas are about an inch long, irregular and two-lipped. HABITAT/RANGE: They prefer dry, rocky, mountain soils and often are found growing in dense, showy, colorful stands, mostly in alpine or subalpine sites from southern British Columbia and western Wyoming to Oregon. Flowers in early summer. FACTS/USES: This is an unusual genus in the figwort family—all the corollas have five stamens. The Greek generic name is derived from *pente*, for five, and *stemon*, meaning stamen. In most species, only four stamens are anther-bearing, with the fifth forming a filament. In some, like this species, the fifth forms a sterile bearded tongue.

SHINING PENSTEMON   *Penstemon nitidus*
This species has several whorls of bright blue flowers on a four- to 12-inch stem. The most distinguishing characteristic of this wildflower is the foliage. The leaves are broadly lanceolate, somewhat thick and fleshy, and have a glaucous or smooth, waxy surface that imparts a whitish or bluish cast to the leaves. Most of the leaves form a basal tuft, with smaller leaves clasping the stem. HABITAT/RANGE: Shining penstemon prefers dry, clayey, exposed soils of plains, hillsides, and slopes, and often can be found on roadsides and other disturbed sites. It is primarily a plains species along the eastern slope of the Rocky Mountains, from Alberta to Saskatchewan, south to Wyoming and Utah. Blooms in spring and early summer. FACTS/USES: The specific name means shining. It is a common and brightly colored early wildflower of the northern plains.

SMALL-FLOWERED PENSTEMON   *Penstemon procerus*
This wildflower also is called clustered penstemon because the corollas are densely clustered in a whorl with open breaks between the whorls. The dark blue or purplish, tubular corollas are small, less than a half-inch long, and slightly two-lipped. The erect stems are four to 20 inches tall with basal, opposite, lanceolate, cauline leaves. HABITAT/RANGE: This plant prefers moist meadows of montane or higher elevations. At alpine levels, the plant becomes dwarfed. It is distributed widely from Alaska to Colorado, but mostly on the eastern mountain ranges. Flowers mostly from early to midsummer. FACTS/USES: The specific name, *procerus*, means tall. This colorful wildflower often is found growing along mountain trails in moist meadows. There are nearly 200 species of penstemons throughout the West and differentiation is difficult.

FLANNEL MULLEIN   *Verbascum thapsus*
Flannel mullein is a biennial herb that produces a dense rosette of thick, very woolly, yellow-green, elliptic leaves its first year. The second year, a robust stalk, covered with red-purple hairs, ascends one to six feet, bearing a dense inflorescence of sulfur-yellow flowers. The one-inch corollas are five-lobed. HABITAT/RANGE: This introduced weed from Europe inhabits disturbed sites in pastures, fields and along roadsides and railroads throughout the temperate United States into southern Canada. Blooms late June through August, but the persistent stalk can remain for several years. FACTS/USES: The dried leaves ignite easily and make excellent fire-starter. Oil-lamp wicks have been made by cutting the leaves into strips. Medicinal uses include relief to asthmatics who smoke the dried leaves and to earache sufferers who use an oil made from the flowers.

AMERICAN SPEEDWELL   *Veronica americana*
A trailing and many-branched plant with creeping rhizomes, the main stem—one to three feet tall—never terminates in an inflorescence. The ovate to lanceolate leaves are opposite, with the small blue flowers in axillary, open racemes. Each flower, only one-quarter-inch long, is four-lobed. HABITAT/RANGE: This plant grows in shallow water or seeps around springs and along streams from lowland to montane. It is a common and widely distributed wildflower throughout North America. Flowers early May through July. FACTS/USES: The derivation of the generic name is not known, but it may have been named for St. Veronica, the woman who used her veil to wipe the perspiration from the forehead of Jesus during the Crucifixion. This plant establishes easily in wet areas along streams and produces dense patches of small blue flowers.

Madder Family
Rubiaceae

NORTHERN BEDSTRAW   *Galium boreale*

A leafy branched plant with four linear to lance-shaped leaves in a whorl at the axils. The stem, six to 24 inches high, is four-angled. Small white, four-petaled, saucer-shaped flowers cluster at the end of branches. HABITAT/RANGE: A common and widespread circumboreal species found in damp or moist open woods from sea level to the mountains, Northern bedstraw blooms from June to August. FACTS/USES: The Greek generic name, *Galium*, may be derived from *galion*—meaning bedstraw. But another definition derives the name *gala*—meaning milk—because it is believed that one species once was used to curdle milk. The common name is derived from its use by Europeans, who dried the sweet-smelling stems and stuffed them into mattress ticking to make a comfortable bed. A purple dye can be made from the roots of some species.

Honeysuckle Family
Caprifoliaceae

TWINFLOWER   *Linnaea borealis*

Two, pink, bell-shaped flowers terminating at the end of an erect, short, four-inch-high, leafy stalk differentiates this species. The stems are slender, woody and trailing, with numerous flower stalks arising from them. Each stalk divides in half near the top, and each pedicel bears a pendulous five-lobed flower. The leaves are broadly elliptic with notches or teeth near the apex. HABITAT/RANGE: This species prefers wet soil along stream banks and seeps of wooded or brushy habitats from low elevations to montane. It is a circumboreal species found within our region in cooler climates across Canada, south to West Virginia, Minnesota, South Dakota, New Mexico and California. Flowers June to September, depending upon elevation. FACTS/USES: The specific name means northern, and the generic name honors the Swedish botanist and taxonomist Carolus Linnæus.

BEARBERRY HONEYSUCKLE   *Lonicera involucrata*

Bearberry honeysuckle is a large, freely branched shrub that can attain a height of three to six feet. Its leaves are opposite, oval in shape, with a pointed tip, dark green, and somewhat hairy along the veins. The distinguishing characteristic is the large, showy, purplish-red, leaflike, hairy bracts above the twin flowers. The yellow flowers are bell-shaped, five-lobed and pendulous beneath the bracts. Each flower matures into a single, glossy, dark purple to black berry with an unpleasant taste. HABITAT/RANGE: It prefers moist sites of springs, stream banks, and canyons, often associated with willows and alders. A widespread cordilleran species occurring from Alaska to New Brunswick, south to Lake Superior, Colorado, Mexico and California. Blooms in early summer, with fruit developing by late summer. FACTS/USES: The specific name means with an involucre, referring to bracts at the base of the flowers.

UTAH HONEYSUCKLE   *Lonicera utahensis*

This bushy shrub can grow two to five feet tall. It bears white to cream-colored, trumpet-shaped flowers, which stem from the leaf axils and hang in pairs. Two bright red berries, sometimes fused together, develop from the swollen base of the flowers. The oval leaves are pale green, somewhat whitish underneath, and smooth. HABITAT/RANGE: Prefers moist soils of open coniferous forests of mid to high elevations and often is associated with lodgepole pine. Utah honeysuckle ranges from British Columbia to Montana, south to New Mexico, Arizona and California. Flowers during spring or early summer and bears fruit by midsummer. FACTS/USES: The generic name honors Adam Lonitzer, a 16th-century German herbalist. The berries contain a toxic alkaloid, saponin, and are poisonous to humans. Small birds and rodents, however, relish the berries.

ELDERBERRY   *Sambucus racemosa*

Elderberry is a highly branched shrub that grows three to 10 feet high. The stems, or branches, are reddish in color and easily broken, exposing a white pith. Clusters of small whitish or cream-colored flowers are borne at the ends of branches in rounded or flat-topped, compound cymes. The opposite leaves on long stalks are pinnately compound in five to seven leaflets. Each leaflet is smooth, pale green, elliptic, and coarsely toothed. The fruit is a berrylike drupe about a quarter inch in diameter and varying in color from bright red, to purple, yellow, black and, occasionally, white. HABITAT/RANGE: Elderberry typically occurs on moist to wet soils along stream banks of woods and canyons up to the montane zone. Distributed from British Columbia to Newfoundland, south to Georgia, Iowa, Colorado and California. Blooms in early summer. FACTS/USES: The specific name means flowers in racemes.

Valerian Family
Valerianaceae

EDIBLE VALERIAN   *Valeriana edulis*

Edible valerian is a tall, erect herb that ascends one to three feet from a stout, fleshy taproot. The stems bear small, whitish flowers clustered in a loosely branched panicle. Tufted basal leaves are thick, oblanceolate, with a few lateral lobed leaves, and nearly parallel veins. HABITAT/RANGE: This species prefers moist sites, especially saline meadows, but also grows on drier open meadows and woodlands. It is distributed widely from British Columbia to Ontario, south to Ohio, New Mexico and Arizona. Blooms May through July. FACTS/USES: The specific name means edible. The large carrot-like root, after cooking, was eaten by the Indians. Although it has a foul odor, described as "dirty feet," cooking does render it palatable. Cats and rats are attracted to the root and, because of this, the root has been used as rat bait.

Harebell Family
Campanulaceae

HAREBELL   *Campanula rotundifolia*

This violet-blue, bell-shaped flower looks awkward on the end of its hairlike stem. The four- to 20-inch stems are not as delicate as they may seem—rather, they are very tough and fibrous. The basal leaves are somewhat round to ovate, while the stem leaves are alternate, long and linear. HABITAT/ RANGE: Harebell prefers dry to moist soils of meadows, open hillsides and rocky slopes of low elevations to timberline. It is a circumboreal species widespread throughout North America, except for the southeast. Flowers June to September, depending on elevation. FACTS/USES: The specific name means round-leaved. The common name is derived from the appearance of the hairlike stem; even old references often spell it as "hairbell." Elevation affects the height and growth of this plant. At lower elevations, it can grow up to 40 inches high but is only a few inches tall at timberline.

Sunflower Family
Asteraceae

YARROW   *Achillea millefolium*

This flower, a perennial herb, can easily be distinguished by its flat top, small white flowers and aromatic fernlike leaves. HABITAT/RANGE: Yarrow is found throughout the Northern Hemisphere and can flourish and prosper in a variety of environments and habitats, including alleys, sagebrush plains, and alpine tundra. Blooms from April to September. FACTS/ USES: The generic name, *Achillea*, is in honor of Achilles, the greatest warrior among the Greeks at Troy and the slayer of Hector. He is credited with first using yarrow as a poultice to cure the wounds of soldiers injured in battle. The odor of its crushed leaves is one of the most outstanding characteristics of yarrow. The leaves when dried and crushed have a strong, aromatic minty smell and are frequently used as a flavoring for tea.

ORANGE AGOSERIS   *Agoseris aurantiaca*

Orange agoseris is a low, 4 to 24 inch high, perennial herb ascending from taproots. One to several stems arise from a basal clump of long, narrow, mostly entire or shallowly toothed leaves. The stem, which when broken produces a milky juice, terminates with a single, orange-red, dandelion-like flower. Each flower head is comprised of all ligulate or ray-like flowers. The seeds, or achenes, are parachute-like when mature. HABITAT/RANGE: This cordilleran species of montane to alpine habitats prefers moist meadows or grassy forest openings. It is a widespread wildflower occurring from British Columbia, Alberta, south to New Mexico and California. Flowers through the summer, depending on elevation. FACTS/USES: The generic name is derived from the Greek *aix*, for goat, and *seris*, for chickory. The specific name means orange-red.

FALSE DANDELION   *Agoseris glauca*
This species is a perennial herb that grows four to 20 inches from a deep taproot. The leaves form a basal cluster varying in shape from long, linear and grasslike to broadly lanceolate, deeply divided and dandelion-like. The stems are unbranched, leafless, produce a milky juice when injured, and terminate with a single yellow flower head comprised of ray flowers. False dandelion is very similar to the true dandelions *(Tarax-acum)* and hawksbeard *(Crepis)*; the main distinguishing characteristics are differences in the seeds. HABITAT/RANGE: They often inhabit somewhat dry to moist flats and meadows of low to mid-mountain elevations. Distributed from British Columbia to Saskatchewan, south to Minnesota, South Dakota, New Mexico and California. Blooms May to early September. FACTS/USES: The specific name means glaucous, or covered with a waxy film.

PEARLY-EVERLASTING   *Anaphalis margaritacea*
Pearly-everlasting is a distinguished-looking flower with numerous, small, but attractive, round, pearly flower heads clustered at the ends of the stem. Each flower is comprised of overlapping, lustrous, papery bracts that look like petals. These surround a small, light yellow center composed of tubular flowers. The stems arise eight to 30 inches from rhizomes and bear grayish, lanceolate leaves with densely hairy undersides. HABITAT/RANGE: It is a widespread plant, preferring dry to moist soils of foothills to almost alpine. As a boreal plant, it is distributed widely in Asia and Europe, and Alaska to Newfoundland, along the East Coast and south to Kansas, New Mexico and California. Blooms through the summer into fall. FACTS/USES: The specific name means pearly. This species is an excellent ornamental herb and dries well for floral arrangements.

ROSY PUSSYTOES   *Antennaria microphylla*
Rosy pussytoes are woolly perennials that form low mats or tufts. The gray-green leaves are mainly basal and oblanceolate. Short stems, two to 12 inches tall, rise above the mat and bear a cluster of flower heads. The heads are composed of numerous, dry, bristly white or rose-colored bracts, the center of which bear inconspicuous disk flowers. This species could be confused with pearly-everlasting *(Anaphalis margaritacea)*, which has pearly or lustrous bracts instead of bristles. HABITAT/RANGE: It prefers grassy or bare sites of open meadows and hillsides of dry to moderately moist soils. It is widespread from Alaska to Saskatchewan, south to New Mexico and California. Blooms May to early August. FACTS/USES: The specific name means small-leaved. The male and female flowers of this species are borne on separate plants.

COMMON BURDOCK *Arctium minus*

This biennial herb produces a rosette of large, wavy, thick, petioled, cordate leaves its first year. During the second year, a robust, highly branched, hairy stalk ascends two to six feet from a large, fleshy taproot. The inflorescence is a raceme with clusters of flower heads that are composed of small red-violet disk flowers surrounded by numerous hooked bracts, which later mature to a round bur. This species is very similar to common cocklebur *(Xanthium strumarium)*, except it is an annual, a native, the leaves are rough and sharp, not as velvety and smooth, and the burs are longer and not as round. HABITAT/RANGE: As a European introduction, it has spread throughout North America and is found on moist pastures, roadsides and ditch banks. It grows from sea level to low mountain elevations. Flowers July to September. FACTS/USES: The specific name means smaller.

HEARTLEAF ARNICA *Arnica cordifolia*

A sunflower-like plant comprised of 10-15 yellow ray and numerous tiny disk flowers in a head often more than two inches wide. The plants have characteristic heart-shaped, toothed, and opposite leaves on a stem eight to 20 inches high. HABITAT/RANGE: A common wildflower growing in patches in moist shaded woods and ascending to timberline, there are 14 species of arnica throughout the West. Heartleaf arnica blooms from May to late July. FACTS/USES: The Latin name, cordifolia, is derived from *cordis*—of the heart, and *folia* —leaves. It is descriptive of the leaf shape and not, as once believed, a medicine for the heart. It is, however, an important medicinal plant. Drugs are prepared from plant extracts and administered to produce a rise in body temperature or cause a mild fever.

BIG SAGEBRUSH *Artemisia tridentata*

Big sagebrush is the most familiar and widespread shrub in the West. This plant is distinguished easily by its large, strap-like, silver-green, three-toothed leaves. It can attain a height of one to seven feet, with the tops projecting spikelike, yellowish, flowering heads. The flowers are small, numerous and inconspicuous. HABITAT/RANGE: It grows on a variety of soils but is intolerant of alkali and inhabits dry plains and hills to timberline. It is distributed widely from British Columbia to North Dakota, New Mexico and California. Flowers late summer and early fall. FACTS/USES: The specific name means three-toothed. This species is not the cooking herb, which is common garden sage *(Salvia officinalis)*, a member of the mint family. Wildlife relish this shrub, but if it is consumed by livestock, the volatile oils can kill digesting microorganisms within their rumen.

ALPINE ASTER *Aster alpigenus*

Alpine aster is a small, graceful flower arising from a simple or slightly branched taproot, and the previous year's vegetation often can be found around its base. Slender, entire margined leaves and several unbranched stems supporting solitary flowering heads arise from this base. The flower heads are comprised of violet or lavender ray flowers with yellow disk flowers in the center. HABITAT/RANGE: Inhabits open, moist meadows at subalpine and alpine habitats and often is found among short, cropped grasses and sedges. Limited in distribution to the central region of the Rocky Mountains, from eastern Oregon to Montana and Wyoming. FACTS/USES: The genus name, *Aster,* is derived from the Greek word for star. The species name means alpine.

SHOWY ASTER *Aster conspicuus*

Showy aster is an erect, leafy, perennial herb ascending from creeping rootstocks and growing up to three feet tall. The stem leaves somewhat clasp the stem and are large and elliptic, with sharply toothed margins. Leaves at the middle of the stem usually are the largest. The flower heads are comprised of 12 to 35 violet or purple ray flowers and yellow disk flowers. The flower heads are individually borne on long stalks and form a flat-topped inflorescence. HABITAT/RANGE: It inhabits moist, rich soils of open woods and often is associated with aspen, conifer stands and old burn areas. It is distributed from the Yukon Territory, British Columbia to Saskatchewan, south to South Dakota, Wyoming and Oregon. Flowers from mid-July to early fall. FACTS/USES: The specific name means conspicuous or showy.

ENGELMANN ASTER *Aster engelmannii*

This species is a large, erect, leafy, perennial herb ascending one to five feet from creeping, underground rootstocks. The leaves are lance-shaped, alternate, pale green with a prominent midrib. The inflorescence bears as many as 20 or more large flower heads. Each is comprised of about 20 large, white ray flowers that turn pinkish or purple with age and have centers of yellow disk flowers. The purplish-tinged involucral bracts are in five rows, with the outer bracts shorter than the inner bracts. HABITAT/RANGE: Engelmann aster often prefers open woods, ranging from foothills to high mountain elevations. It is found from British Columbia to Alberta, south to Colorado and northeast Nevada. Blooms mid-July until late September. FACTS/USES: The specific name honors Dr. George Engelmann, a 19th-century American botanist.

THICKSTEM ASTER   *Aster integrifolius*

Thickstem aster is a leafy, perennial forb ascending eight to 20 inches from a stout rootstock. The reddish stems are somewhat glabrous at the base and glandular-hairy at the top into the inflorescence. Basal leaves are large, narrow, lance-shaped, entire, wavy and taper to a winged stalk, while the upper leaves are oblong, stalkless and somewhat clasp the stem. The flower heads clustered at the end of the stem have a ragged appearance. Each flower head has 10 to 27 deep bluish-purple ray flowers with a small center of yellow disk flowers. HABITAT/RANGE: This species prefers dry meadows, hillsides and open woods of mid-elevations and often is associated with goldenrod and lupine. It is well-distributed from Washington to Montana, south to Colorado and California. Flowers mid-July through fall. FACTS/USES: The specific name means entire-leaved.

ARROWLEAF BALSAMROOT   *Balsamorhiza sagittata*

Arrowleaf balsamroot is a robust, perennial herb that attains a height of eight to 36 inches. It is recognized easily by its large, showy, yellow flower heads and silvery-green, arrow-shaped leaves. HABITAT/RANGE: It prefers well-drained soils, southern exposures and open ridges of foothills to mid-mountain elevations. This species is well-distributed from British Columbia to Saskatchewan, south to Colorado and central California, but east of the Cascade Mountains. Blooms May to early July. FACTS/USES: The specific name means arrow-like, referring to the leaf shape. The common and generic name is derived from its thick, resinous *(balsam)* roots *(rhiza)*. The roasted seeds can be ground into a flour, called pinole. The Nez Perce Indians were known to roast and grind the seeds, which they then formed into little balls by adding grease.

NODDING BEGGARS-TICK   *Bidens cernua*

Nodding beggars-tick has bright yellow flower heads one to two inches in diameter with as many as 12 ray flowers. There are two distinct rows of green involucral bracts. One main distinguishing characteristic is the leaves, which are opposite, lanceolate, sharply toothed and may clasp or join around the stem. Another characteristic is the seeds, which are small and flattened with two projecting spines covered with backward-pointing barbs. HABITAT/RANGE: This species often is found along the edges of ponds or other wet, boggy soils of low to mid-mountain elevations. It is distributed widely throughout North America from British Columbia to New Brunswick, south to North Carolina, Missouri, New Mexico and California. Flowers July to September. FACTS/USES: The Latin generic name means two teeth and refers to the spines. The specific name means drooping or nodding.

MUSK THISTLE   *Carduus nutans*

This large, branching biennial reaches a height of one to nine feet. The leaves are deeply lobed and jagged, with sharp spines. The leaf stems are winged (decurrent) and generally run down the stalk. The large, two- to three-inch-wide, deep lavender, rayless heads nod on the stem. The involucral bracts are conspicuous, sharp and stiff, with the lower ones bent back. HABITAT/RANGE: Introduced from Eurasia, it is found sparingly throughout the United States and into Canada. It establishes easily on disturbed sites, especially along roads. A summer and fall bloomer. FACTS/USES: The generic name, *Carduus*, is the Latin word for thistle. The specific name, *nutans*, means nodding, and refers to the nodding or drooping heads. The large and colorful heads are attractants for pollinating insects and small animals.

SPOTTED KNAPWEED   *Centaurea maculosa*

Knapweed is a biennial herb or short-lived perennial that produces a rosette of long, deeply pinnate leaves. In its second year, the taproot sends up a branching leafy stem one to three feet tall. The numerous pinkish or purple flower heads are arranged at the ends of terminal and branching stems. The ray flowers are finely and narrowly segmented, and the involucral bracts have dark, finely fringed tips. HABITAT/ RANGE: This plant prefers dry, gravelly or sandy soils of disturbed sites, especially along roadsides and overgrazed pastures. Introduced and naturalized from Europe, it has established throughout western North America. Flowers through the summer into fall. FACTS/USES: The specific name means spotted. Knapweed is an aggressive, competitive plant, establishing quickly on disturbed sites and producing a chemical to inhibit surrounding plants.

DUSTY MAIDEN   *Chaenactis alpina*

Dusty maiden is a perennial, taprooted herb. The white or pinkish flower heads lack ray flowers; instead, they are comprised of showy, tubular disk flowers, giving the appearance of ray flowers. The four- to 18-inch stem is openly branched, with a flower head terminating at the end of each branch. The stem also is very leafy and bears deeply dissected, fernlike leaves that are lightly woolly with a dusty look. Larger leaves form a rosette at the base. This species could be confused with yarrow *(Achillea millefolium)*, which does have ray flowers. HABITAT/RANGE: Commonly grows on dry, gravelly or sandy soils of mountain ridges, hillsides and disturbed sites of mid-mountain to alpine elevations. Distributed from British Columbia to Montana, south to New Mexico and California, it flowers through the summer. FACTS/USES: The specific name honors botanist David Douglas.

HAIRY GOLDEN ASTER   *Chrysopsis villosa*

This is a short eight- to 20-inch grayish-hairy plant with several leafy, ascending or spreading stems. The numerous lanceolate leaves are petioled, except for the upper ones. The yellow inch-broad flowers have 10-25 ray flowers surrounding the golden disk. HABITAT/RANGE: A widespread plant of dry, sandy riverbottoms, roadsides, and open areas of foothills into the lower montane. Distributed from British Columbia to Wisconsin, Nebraska, south to Texas, Mexico and California. Flowers early June into September. FACTS/USES: The generic name, *Chrysopsis*, is derived from the Greek words *chrysos*, meaning gold, and *opis*, meaning aspect, and refers to the color of the heads. The specific name, *villosa*, means soft-hairy, referring to the soft pubescence covering the stem and leaves.

RABBITBRUSH   *Chrysothamnus nauseosus*

This shrub has golden-yellow flowers borne in a dense cluster on the ends of each stem, giving the stems a whiskbroom appearance. The flowers, lacking ray flowers, are composed entirely of yellow disk flowers. The stem is silver, due to a dense mat of white, woolly hairs, while the leaves are linear, narrow and green. HABITAT/RANGE: Rabbitbrush prefers dry, sandy, gravelly or clayey soils of open desert plains and foothills to mid-mountain elevations. It is distributed east of the Cascade Mountains to Alberta, south to Texas and Mexico. Flowers late summer through fall. FACTS/USES: The specific name means nauseous and refers to the distasteful flavor of the herbage to livestock. This species contains a high-grade rubber compound called chrysil. The flowers and stems produce a bright yellow dye.

CANADA THISTLE   *Cirsium arvense*

This perennial herb has deep or extensively creeping rootstocks. The stems, rising one to four feet high, are grooved and branch only at the top. The lavender or rose-purple heads are dioecious (male and female flower usually in separate heads and borne on different plants) and measure less than one inch wide. HABITAT/RANGE: A cosmopolitan flower introduced from Eurasia, it invades disturbed fields, pastures and roadsides. It is found extensively throughout Canada and extends as far south as central California and Iowa. Blooms late June into early August. FACTS/USES: The specific name, *arvense*, means pertaining to cultivated fields, referring to its characteristic habit of invading disturbed pastures and producing dense patches.

ELK THISTLE   *Cirsium scariosum*

Elk thistle has large, spiny, grayish-green leaves attached to a thick stalk, which may stand anywhere from four inches to four feet tall. The light lavender flowers are hidden and clumped among the foliage near the top. HABITAT/RANGE: Prefers meadows and other moist soils from foothills to montane and subalpine zones. It is a common plant from British Columbia to Saskatchewan south to New Mexico and California. Blooms June to early August. FACTS/USES: Elk thistle, also know as Everts' thistle, saved the life of Truman Everts in Yellowstone National Park in 1870. Everts, an explorer, became separated from his group and his horse for 37 days. Because a botanist had remarked that the root of this plant was edible and nutritious, it was the only plant he knew was safe to eat, and he subsisted on the raw root.

BULL THISTLE   *Cirsium vulgare*

This biennial herb reproduces by seeds. The first year, a rosette of coarsely toothed, lanceolate leaves appears. By the second year, a stout one- to six-foot stalk arises from the taproot. The leaves are deeply cut with long, needle-pointed spines, and the upper surface of the leaf is covered with short, stiff hairs. The flower heads, deep-purple to rose-colored, are one to two inches wide. HABITAT/RANGE: Bull thistle is an introduced and naturalized plant from Eurasia, now found throughout the United States and north into Canada, from British Columbia to Newfoundland. An invader of pastures and other disturbed sites, it is a late summer and early fall bloomer. FACTS/USES: The generic name, *Cirsium*, is derived from the Greek word *kirsos*, which means a swollen vein for which thistles were used as a remedy.

HAWKSBEARD   *Crepis acuminata*

Hawksbeard is a perennial, milky-juiced herb that attains a height of eight to 30 inches. The yellow flower heads are numerous, 20 to 100 in large robust plants, and clustered on the ends of branches, forming a flat or roundish top. Each flower head is composed of five or six flowers. The leaves are mainly basal, or low on the stem, and are long, slightly hairy, and pinnately dissected into linear or sharp-toothed lobes. HABITAT/RANGE: This plant prefers well-drained, often stony soils and open hillsides of sagebrush plains to coniferous forests. Often associated with arrowleaf balsamroot, it is distributed widely from British Columbia to Alberta, south to New Mexico and eastern California. Blooms late May until August. FACTS/USES: The specific name means acuminate, long-pointed or tapering, and refers to the leaf tip.

LOW HAWKSBEARD   *Crepis modocensis*

Low hawksbeard is a small, four- to 12-inch-tall, milky-juiced perennial herb. The dandelion-like flowers are yellow with an involucre made up of a single series of long, sepal-like bracts. There are only one to nine flower heads composed of five-toothed, petallike ray flowers. The leaves are long, lance-shape in outline and deeply dissected into linear or sharp-toothed lobes. HABITAT/RANGE: Grows on well-drained, gravelly soils of open flats or hillsides among sagebrush or coniferous forests. Distributed from southern British Columbia to Montana, south to Colorado and Oregon. Flowers May through July. FACTS/USES: The common name of hawksbeard refers to the bristly, pappus hairs of the seed, resembling the bristles on the side of a hawk's beak. The specific name is derived from the Greek word *krepis*, which means boot or sandal, the reference to which is obscure.

CUTLEAF DAISY   *Erigeron compositus*

The small, delicate, half-inch- to one-inch-diameter flower heads are supported on slender stems that are less than a foot tall. Each flower head is composed of numerous yellow disk flowers with delicate, fine, white, pinkish or blue ray flowers. The leaves help distinguish this species from others. They form a basal cluster and are highly dissected into threes, with narrow, fingerlike lobes. HABITAT/RANGE: Prefers dry, gravelly, or rocky sites of low- or mid- to high-mountain elevations. It is widespread in cooler climates across Canada and Greenland, south to Quebec, Colorado, Arizona and California. Blooms early spring to midsummer. FACTS/USES: The specific name means compound. Daisies or fleabanes can be difficult to separate from asters. One distinguishing feature is the involucral bracts around the flower heads. Daisies have one or two series or rows of bracts, while asters have two, three or more rows overlapping like shingles.

SPREADING FLEABANE   *Erigeron divergens*

Spreading fleabane is a widely branched biennial or short-lived perennial that attains a height of four to 28 inches. The foliage and stems are covered with short, grayish hairs. The leaves are oblanceolate or spatulate, the largest clustered at the bottom and the stem leaves reduced in size. A one-inch diameter flower head borne at the end of each branch has a yellow disk flower center and numerous white, pinkish, or lavender ray flowers. HABITAT/RANGE: This species typically occurs on dry waste areas of plains, valleys and foothills. It is distributed widely from British Columbia, east of the Cascades, to Montana, south to Texas and California. Flowers April to August. FACTS/USES: The specific name means widespreading. The common name of fleabane came from Europe, where members of this genus either were burned or hung in cottages as a flea repellent.

SHOWY FLEABANE *Erigeron speciosus*

As its common name implies, this is one of the showiest, most colorful and widespread fleabanes of the West. One to several flower heads are borne on short stalks arising from leaf axils and forming a somewhat flat-topped arrangement. Each flower head is one to two inches in diameter and composed of yellow, tubular disk flowers and narrow, linear, lilac to bluish-purple ray flowers. The involucral bracts are in two rows, narrow and finely granular. The leafy stems are erect and usually one to three feet tall. Leaves are alternate, entire with conspicuous hairs along the margin, and the upper leaves somewhat clasp the stem. HABITAT/RANGE: Showy fleabane inhabits moist, open meadows, woods and burned sites of coniferous forests. Distributed from British Columbia to Alberta, south to New Mexico and California. Blooms June to August. FACTS/USES: The specific name means showy or good-looking.

WOOLLY SUNFLOWER *Eriophyllum lanatum*

This species is a small, usually clumped, perennial herb with golden-yellow flower heads. The erect stems, four to 24 inches tall, are leafy and covered with dense, white, woolly hairs, giving the plant a gray appearance. Each stem is branched and bears a flower head of eight to 12 broad, yellow ray flowers and yellow disk flowers. The fruit is a slender, four-angled achene. HABITAT/RANGE: Woolly sunflower prefers dry, open, often sandy or gravelly soils of ridges or roadsides of foothills to mountain slopes. It typically occurs from British Columbia to Western Montana, south to Utah and southern California. Flowers May through July. FACTS/USES: The generic name is derived from the Greek words *erion*, for wool, and *phyllon*, for foliage, and refers to the dense, gray, woolly stems and leaves. The specific name also means woolly.

BLANKET-FLOWER *Gaillardia aristata*

This perennial herb ascends six to 24 inches from slender taproots. Each hairy stem has a terminal, large, showy, flowering head two to three inches wide, with bright yellow, three-lobed ray flowers, which sometimes are reddish at the base. The disk flowers are reddish or purple and domelike. The lance-shaped leaves are mostly basal, oblong and entire to coarsely toothed. HABITAT/RANGE: Often found growing in small clumps on sunny and well-drained plains and rocky slopes of the grasslands into the montane zone. Distributed from British Columbia to Saskatchewan, south to New Mexico and Arizona. Blooms June to early August. FACTS/USES: The specific name, *aristata*, means bearded, referring to the hairy stem and lower leaves. Blanket-flower is a popular transplant to domestic gardens, where it commonly is known as brown-eyed Susan.

CURLYCUP GUMWEED   *Grindelia squarrosa*

Gumweed is a native, perennial (sometimes biennial) forb with branching stems reaching one to three feet high. Numerous, oblong, slightly toothed leaves clasp the stem and twist, giving the plant a ragged appearance. The inch-wide yellow flower heads are composed of 25-40 bright yellow ray flowers and dark-colored disk flowers. The distinguishing characteristic of this plant is that the flower head is surrounded by small, upward-curving bracts that exude a sticky substance. HABITAT/RANGE: Distributed from British Columbia to Minnesota, Nebraska, Texas and California on arid and disturbed rangelands. A late summer bloomer, from July through September. FACTS/USES: The generic name means with parts spreading, referring to the curving bracts of the head. The Indians used this medicinal plant for colic, indigestion, consumption, and throat and lung troubles.

BROOM SNAKEWEED   *Gutierrezia sarothrae*

Broom snakeweed is a perennial shrub with diffusely branching, woody stems. The stems do not regrow from the previous year's growth, but regrow from the crown. The numerous, slender, erect stems give the appearance of a broom. Alternate, narrow, resinous-sticky leaves follow the stem. At the end of each stem is a cluster of small, yellow flower heads arranged in a loose, flat-topped cyme. HABITAT/RANGE: This plant commonly inhabits dry, well-drained, sandy or gravelly soils of open plains, foothills and mountain slopes. It is considered a Great Plains species, distributed from Alberta to Manitoba, south to western Texas, southern California, Nevada and Idaho. Flowers July to September. FACTS/USES: The specific name is derived from the Latin word *sarothrum*, which means broom. The generic name comes from Piedro Gutierrez, a Spanish botanist of the early 19th century.

STEMLESS GOLDENWEED   *Haplopappus acaulis*

Stemless goldenweed is a small, herbaceous perennial that grows in dense patches. Its basal leaves are dark green, narrow, and stiff or rough to the touch. Numerous, nearly leafless stalks arise up to six inches from the dense tufts. Each stalk bears a single, yellow flower head, about an inch and a half in diameter, with six to 15 ray flowers. HABITAT/RANGE: A dweller of dry, open sites of foothills and valleys to high mountain elevations, it is a widespread plant, found from Idaho to Saskatchewan, south to Colorado and California. Flowers May to July. FACTS/USES: The generic name is derived from the Greek words *haplous*, for simple, and *pappos*, for seed down, and refers to the single series of unbranched, bristle-like hairs or pappi surmounting the achene. The specific name means stemless.

ONE-FLOWERED GOLDENWEED   *Haplopappus uniflorus*
This perennial herb ascends eight to 12 inches from a branching, somewhat woody rootstock. Each erect, leafy, reddish stem, often with a loose cottony coating, bears a single flower head composed of yellow ray and disk flowers. The stem and basal leaves are lanceolate and often have sharply dentate margins. HABITAT/RANGE: This species prefers moist to wet, sandy, sometimes alkaline soils of river terraces, open meadows and stream banks of foothills to mid-mountain elevations. It is especially found on the geyser formations in Yellowstone National Park but is not widely distributed in the West. It is found from Oregon, central Idaho to Saskatchewan, south to Colorado and California. Flowers May to July. FACTS/USES: The specific name means one-flowered. Members of this genus are difficult to distinguish. They differ so greatly that some botanists have separated them into several distinct genera.

LITTLE-SUNFLOWER   *Helianthella uniflora*
Little-sunflower is a common wildflower that can be differentiated from its close relatives—showy goldeneye *(Viguiera multiflora)* and common sunflower *(Helianthus annuus)* mainly by the seeds. Little-sunflower seeds are flat, with narrow-winged edges and a notch on the top, while the others have round or four-angled seeds. This perennial herb grows one to two feet tall from a tough, woody rootcrown. Numerous leafy stems bear a solitary, yellow flower head. The lanceolate leaves have fine, stiff hairs and often have a prominent three-nerved vein. HABITAT/RANGE: It prefers moderately rich soils of hillsides and open woods at low to high mountain elevations. Widely distributed east of the Cascade Mountains in Washington to Montana, south to New Mexico and Arizona. Flowers early to late summer. FACTS/USES: The specific name means single-flowered.

COMMON SUNFLOWER   *Helianthus annuus*
Common sunflower is a robust, leafy annual that can attain a height of one to eight feet. The leaves are very rough, ovate or even heart-shaped, with irregular-toothed margins. Flowering heads usually are solitary and three to five inches in diameter, with bright yellow ray flowers and dark brown or purplish disk flowers. This native Western species has been cultivated and hybridized into highly colored, gigantic garden varieties. HABITAT/RANGE: Prefers open, dry to moderately moist soils along roads and foothills throughout most of North America. Flowers June to September. FACTS/USES: The generic name is derived from the Greek words *helios*, for sun, and *anthos*, for flower. The specific name means annual. The dark gray seeds are a popular product of this plant and are eaten roasted or as an oil extract. It is the state flower of Kansas.

WHITE-FLOWERED HAWKWEED   *Hieracium albiflorum*
White-flowered hawkweed is a perennial herb with large basal and smaller, alternate leaves on the stems. The leaves are entire or slightly toothed, oblong or oblanceolate and sparsely covered with long white hairs. The one- to three-foot stems terminate in an open-branched cyme. The flower heads usually number from 15 to 30 and are composed of white or cream-colored ray flowers. HABITAT/RANGE: This species grows in dry to moderately moist, open-wooded slopes of foothills to mountains. It is a cordilleran species distributed from Alaska to Saskatchewan, south to New Mexico and California. Flowers late June to early August. FACTS/USES: The specific name means white-flowered. The generic name is derived from the Greek word *hierax*, for hawk. Indians used the coagulated juice of this plant as a chewing gum.

STEMLESS HYMENOXYS　　　　　*Hymenoxys acaulis*
Stemless hymenoxys is an unusual flower, in that it lacks true stems. Each solitary flower terminates at the end of a leafless flower stalk that grows up to a foot tall. The stout taproots generally are divided, and each crown often has the previous year's withered foliage and a single flower stalk. New leaves are clustered at the base and are linear to oblanceolate with dense hairs. The bright yellow flower heads have three-toothed ray flowers and numerous tubular disk flowers. HABITAT/RANGE: It is a widespread wildflower on dry soils of high plains to above timberline. Stemless hymenoxys is distributed from Idaho to central Canada and Ohio, south to Texas and California. Flowers June to September. FACTS/USES: The specific name is derived from the Greek prefix *a*, which means not, and *kaulos*, for stem.

OLD-MAN-OF-THE-MOUNTAIN   *Hymenoxys grandiflora*
This is a grayish-green, tomentose plant of the mountain summits. The leaves are finely dissected into fingerlike projections and are mainly basal. Several hairy stalks arise one to 12 inches from the taproots, and each stem terminates with a solitary flower head. The flower heads are showy, with 20 or more yellow ray flowers and a broad disk. HABITAT/RANGE: This mountain species prefers talus slopes, windswept ridges, and rocky or gravelly sites of high elevations. It occurs from central Idaho to southwest Montana and from Colorado to Utah. Blooms June to August, depending upon elevation. FACTS/USES: The generic name, *hymenoxys*, is derived from the Greek word *hymen*, for membrane, and *oxys*, for sharp, in reference to the thin pappus. The specific name means large-flowered.

GAYFEATHER   *Liatris punctata*

Gayfeather is a warm-season, perennial forb that produces a taproot-like corm, which may reach 15 feet deep. It is easily distinguished by its brilliant purple, flowered spike. The stems are unbranched and attain a height of one to two feet. The numerous, linear leaves almost hide the stem and are covered with small dots or glands. HABITAT/RANGE: It typically prefers dry, shallow, sandy or loamy soils of open prairies and foothills. This species is found mainly on the Great Plains from Manitoba to Texas, but extends west along the east slope of the Rocky Mountains. Flowers midsummer to late fall. FACTS/USES: The specific name means punctate or dotted. The large bulb-like root has a carroty flavor and was cooked or eaten raw by Indians. The root also has medicinal uses, such as an infusion to cure an itch or a tea for blood in the urine or vague female ills.

BLUE LETTUCE   *Lactuca pulchella*

Blue lettuce is a perennial herb that reproduces by seed or from an extensive taproot system. The erect, tall, eight- to 40-inch stem usually is branched and leafy up to the inflorescence. The alternate leaves are thick with lance-shaped upper leaves and lower leaves that are merely a narrow, lobed wing. When either the stem or foliage is broken, it produces a milky juice. The small, blue ray-flowered heads are arranged in an open panicle. HABITAT/RANGE: This native plant establishes well in meadows, sagebrush plains, along stream courses and roadsides. Blue lettuce is distributed from British Columbia to Michigan, south to Kansas, southern New Mexico, and central California. Flowers through the summer. FACTS/USES: The generic name is derived from the Latin word *Lac*, for milk, and refers to the milky juice. The specific name means pretty or beautiful.

CONEFLOWER   *Ratibida columnifera*

This perennial herb ascends one to four feet high from taproots. The flower heads are borne singly on the ends of branched stems. Each flower head has a brownish, cylindrical, or thimble-shaped, disk nearly two inches long, with three to seven drooping, yellow ray flowers. The leaves are narrow or divided in five, seven or nine long, narrow segments. HABITAT/RANGE: Commonly occurring on dry to moist soils of open plains, prairies and foothills, this Great Plains species extends west along the eastern slopes of the Rocky Mountains and north to Alberta and south to Mexico. Blooms July to September. FACTS/USES: The specific name means columnar, referring to the cone-shaped flower head. Indians used the flower heads to produce a yellow-orange dye. A pleasant tea can be brewed from the leaves and flowers. The roots of some *Ratibida* species have been known to cure toothaches.

WESTERN CONEFLOWER   *Rudbeckia occidentalis*
Western coneflower is easily recognized by the tall, two- to
five-foot, leafy stems with one or several cylindrical, dark
brown heads. The flower lacks the bright-colored ray flowers
common on most sunflowers. Instead, this species has developed a large cone-shaped head one to two inches in diameter, with a series of leafy bracts around the base. The head
is entirely composed of hundreds of small disk flowers that
begin blooming at the bottom and progress spirally toward the
top, where they form a halo of tiny, bright yellow flowers. The
leaves are egg-shaped, tapered at the tip and somewhat
toothed. HABITAT/RANGE: It grows in moist soils of open or
shaded stream banks, hillsides and woods, often preferring
aspen stands. Occurs from Washington to Montana, Colorado and California. Flowers late June through August. FACTS/
USES: The specific name means Western.

WESTERN GROUNDSEL   *Senecio integerrimus*
This tall, usually single-stemmed, perennial herb ascends 12
to 40 inches from a short-lived rootcrown with fibrous roots.
The leafy stems bear small, narrow, lanceolate or linear
leaves, while leaves on the lower portion have a variety of
shapes, from obovate to oblanceolate. The small, numerous
flower heads are about a half inch in diameter and are borne
in a terminal cluster. Each flower head is composed of yellow
ray and disk flowers. The seeds are glabrous but have a
crown of bristle-like hairs, which is a characteristic of the
groundsels. HABITAT/RANGE: A widespread plant preferring sagebrush and ponderosa pine belts of valleys to timberline, Western groundsel is a variable species distributed
throughout the Great Plains region and through the Rocky
Mountains from British Columbia to Colorado. FACTS/USES:
The specific name means very entire, referring to the leaf
margin.

ARROWLEAF GROUNDSEL   *Senecio triangularis*
Arrowleaf groundsel is a tall, leafy perennial with fleshy
compact rootstocks. The stout, leafy stems grow one to six
feet tall and terminate in a cluster of flower heads arranged in
a flat-topped cyme. Each one-inch-diameter flower head is
composed of yellow disk flowers and six to 12 yellow ray
flowers. This species often is confused with butterweed
groundsel *(S. serra)*, which has lanceolate or egg-shaped
leaves with saw-toothed margins. Arrowleaf groundsel has
characteristic wedge-shaped or arrow-shaped leaves with
saw-toothed margins. HABITAT/RANGE: This plant prefers
cooler sites and moist, rich soils along streams or meadows
of low to high elevations. It is distributed from Alaska to
Saskatchewan, south to New Mexico and California. Flowers
during July and August, with seed development in September. FACTS/USES: Both the specific and common names
refer to the leaf shape.

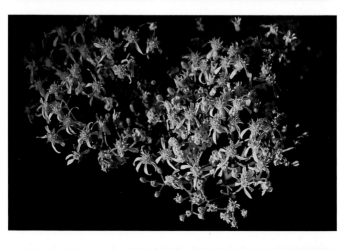

MISSOURI GOLDENROD   *Solidago missouriensis*

Missouri goldenrod is an erect, perennial herb ascending eight to 36 inches from a well-developed creeping rhizome. The small, yellow flower heads are arranged on one side of the spreading branches in a densely clustered inflorescence. Each flower head contains ray and disk flowers, usually with eight—or occasionally up to 13—ray flowers. The lanceolate, smooth and entire leaves are arranged alternately along the stem. HABITAT/RANGE: It prefers dry, often gravelly, open sites of plains, valley and high-mountain elevations. It is a Great Plains dweller distributed from southern British Columbia to Wisconsin, south to Missouri, Oklahoma, and Arizona. Flowers July to September. FACTS/USES: The generic name is derived from the Latin names *solidus* and *ago*, meaning to make whole, and refers to its medicinal healing properties.

PRICKLY SOW-THISTLE   *Sonchus asper*

This species is an annual herb with a short taproot. The one- to five-foot, leafy stems produce a milky juice when injured, and the stems are smooth with a waxy, powdery surface. The leaves are crowded along the stem and vary in shape from scarcely lobed to deeply lobed with prickly toothed margins. The one-half-inch to one-inch diameter, pale-yellow flower heads are composed entirely of ray flowers. HABITAT/RANGE: As an introduced plant from Eurasia, it has established throughout the United States in orchards, grainfields and other cultivated or disturbed sites. Flowers late June until frost, and flowers during the winter in southern climates. FACTS/USES: The specific name means rough. Young stems and leaves can be used for greens. A related species, *(S. oleraceus)*, has been used to derive a gum used to treat opium addiction.

COMMON TANSY   *Tanacetum vulgare*

Common tansy is an aromatic, robust, perennial herb that attains a height of one to six feet. It can reproduce from either seeds or rootstalks. The most distinguishing characteristics are bright yellow, button-like flowers clustered in a dense corymb and alternate, pinnately compound leaves, finely dissected into numerous, narrow, toothed segments. HABITAT/RANGE: This naturalized plant from Eurasia was introduced as an ornamental but has escaped cultivation and now inhabits disturbed sites, especially roadsides throughout North America. Blooms late summer through fall. FACTS/USES: The specific name means vulgar or common. This species is well-known for its medicinal uses, which include soaking the leaves in buttermilk for nine days to make a skin lotion; making a brew from the leaves to induce natural menstruation; or making a soothing tea.

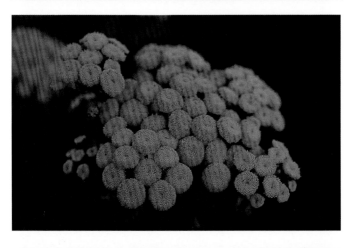

COMMON DANDELION
Taraxacum officinale

The common dandelion probably is the best-known and widespread "weed" in the world. Leafless, hollow stems ascend from a thick taproot and bear a single flower head composed entirely of yellow ray flowers. The leaves are all basal, forming a rosette, and are long, deeply cut and lobed. As the flower head matures, the receptacle develops numerous achenes, each with an umbrella-shaped plume, forming a seed head or ball. HABITAT/RANGE: This species prefers moist soils; it can be found in meadows, pastures and stream banks from sea level to high mountains. It is a circumboreal and introduced plant found throughout North America. Flowers April to October, depending upon elevation. FACTS/USES: The dandelion is known to have hundreds of medicinal values and was given the specific name of *officinale*, meaning official, because of its importance as a drug plant. The leaves make excellent salad greens.

GRAY HORSEBRUSH
Tetradymia canescens

Horsebrush is a highly branched, woody shrub two to three feet tall, with numerous tubular flower heads. The flower heads are characteristic in that they consist of four yellow disk flowers enclosed in four stiff, grayish, tomentose scales. Most of the lower stems are woody and lack leaves. The outer new growth has linear or oblanceolate, gray and densely tomentose leaves. HABITAT/RANGE: This species prefers dry, rocky or sandy soils of plains and foothills to low mountain elevations. It is distributed from British Columbia, east of the Cascade Mountains, to Montana, south to New Mexico and southern California. Flowers June to early September. FACTS/USES: The generic name is derived from the Greek word *tetradymos*, which means fourfold and refers to the four flowers and bracts. The specific name means gray-pubescent. Indians are reputed to have used the root for female maladies.

MOUNTAIN TOWNSENDIA
Townsendia alpigena

Mountain townsendia is a small, perennial herb with a branching root crown and a dense cluster of small, white-hairy, spatulate leaves. The one-inch-diameter flower heads rise only two inches above the ground and are showy with purple or lavender ray flowers and yellow disk flowers. This species often is confused with alpine aster *(Aster alpigenus)*, which has slender, grasslike leaves. HABITAT/RANGE: This subalpine species prefers gravelly, windswept ridges or mountain summits. It is a widespread cordilleran species from British Columbia to Colorado. Blooms July and August. FACTS/USES: The specific name means alpine. Townsendias are difficult to distinguish from asters *(Aster)* and fleabanes *(Erigeron)*. Townsendias have large flower heads in proportion to the plant and long, flat scales on top of the seeds, while asters and daisies have round, hairlike bristles.

PARRY'S TOWNSENDIA   *Townsendia parryi*

The most distinguishing characteristic of this alpine flower is the size of the flower heads, which are about two inches in diameter and are large in proportion to the plant. They have blue-lavender ray flowers with yellow disk flowers. This short-lived perennial with a small taproot has one to several leafy flower stalks up to a foot tall. Leaves are spatulate in shape, somewhat hairy, mostly basal with the stem leaves decreasing in size toward the flower head. This species easily could be confused with *T. incana*, a southern Rockies species, or alpine daisy *(Erigeron simplex)*. HABITAT/RANGE: This montane or subalpine plant, which mostly is found on open, gravelly soils, is a cordilleran species distributed from Washington to Alberta, south to Colorado. Blooms during midsummer. FACTS/USES: The generic name honors David Townsend, the 19th-century botanist who first described this plant.

MEADOW SALSIFY   *Tragopogon pratensis*

This perennial herb ascends one to four feet from taproots. The stems are hollow and produce a milky juice when cut. The grasslike leaves clasp the stem and, at the end of each stalk, is a pale yellow flower head. Each flower is comprised of numerous ray flowers surrounded by long, pointed green bracts. The flowers mature into large, round conspicuous seed heads, with each individual seed attached to a parachute-shaped plume. HABITAT/RANGE: This species prefers moist habitats, especially mountain meadows and roadsides. Blooms early to late summer. A related and common species, yellow salsify *(T. dubius)*, is more adapted to lowlands and drier sites. Both species have European origin and are widespread throughout the West. FACTS/USES: The generic name means of meadows. The roots are edible and have a parsnip taste.

SHOWY GOLDENEYE   *Viguiera multiflora*

Goldeneye is a tall, perennial herb, up to four feet in height. The stems are highly branched and bear numerous brilliant yellow-gold flowers. Each flower head is composed of 10 to 14 ray flowers that are nearly an inch long with a dark golden center, giving the appearance of a "goldeneye." The leaves are opposite, lance-shaped and slightly toothed. This species could be confused with golden aster *(Chrysopsis villosa)*. HABITAT/RANGE: It generally prefers dry, open hillsides and road edges of foothills to subalpine zones. Well-distributed in the central Rocky Mountains, from Washington to southwest Montana, south to New Mexico and California, it flowers through the summer, from July to September. FACTS/USES: The specific name means many-flowered. The genus is named in honor of Dr. L.G.A. Viguier, a French physician, librarian and botanist.

MULE'S-EARS   *Wyethia amplexicaulis*

Mule's-ears is appropriately named because its leaves are shaped like the ears of a mule. The leaves are dark green, smooth, crisp and leathery with a waxy or resinous covering. The plants often grow in large patches or clumps. A stout, leafy stem one to two feet tall ascends from a thickened, woody taproot. The stems terminate with a single, bright yellow flower head. This species could be confused with arrowleaf balsamroot *(Balsamorhiza sagittata)*, which has grayish, arrow-shaped basal leaves. HABITAT/RANGE: Mule's-ears grows on dry, open flats or hillsides of foothills to mid-mountain elevations. It is distributed widely, from British Columbia to Montana, south to Colorado, Nevada and Oregon. Flowers May to July, depending upon elevation. FACTS/USES: The specific name means stem-clasping. Indians cooked the taproots in a stone pit for one or two days to ferment them.

WHITE WYETHIA   *Wyethia helianthoides*

This stout, leafy, perennial forb closely resembles a related species, mule's-ears. It differs in that it has short, stiff hairs on the foliage, larger white or cream-colored flower heads and usually is not as tall. HABITAT/RANGE: White wyethia typically grows in moist or wet, open meadows of low to mid-mountain elevations. When in bloom, they often cover large grassy meadows, fields or dense patches with their white blossoms. It has a small distribution from Washington, east of the Cascades, to Montana, Wyoming and Oregon. Flowers from May until early July. FACTS/USES: The generic name, *Wyethia*, honors Captain Nathaniel Wyeth, an explorer who traveled through the West in 1834 with English naturalist and botanist Thomas Nuttall. Wyeth was the first to collect and describe this genus, which occurs only in western North America.

Peony Family
Paeonia brownii

BROWN'S PEONY   *Paeonia brownii*

Growing in clumps eight to 20 inches high, the large, leathery, dissected, bluish-green leaves often hide the pendulous flowers. The flowers, one to two inches wide, tend not to open widely to reveal five unequal greenish sepals, the reddish-brown petals and the densely packed yellow anthers. When the flower begins to fruit, five large pod-like follicles appear. HABITAT/RANGE: This rare and infrequent wildflower blooms in sagebrush desert to cottonwood riparian and ponderosa pine forests from May until late June. It is found from eastern Washington to western Wyoming, south to Utah and south-central California. FACTS/USES: The generic, *Paeonia*, is a Greek name commemorating Paeon, the physician of the Gods, who is believed to have used this plant medicinally. The roots, used by Native Americans, have a licorice taste.

A KEY TO THE FAMILIES

(Adapted from *Flora of the Pacific Northwest* by C. Leo Hitchcock and Arthur Cronquist)

1a Embryo generally with one cotyledon; leaves generally parallel-veined; floral parts generally borne in sets of 3, seldom 4, never 5; herbs ....**Liliopsida** (Monocots), lead 2a

1b Embryo generally with two cotyledons; leaves generally pinnately or palmately veined; floral parts generally borne in sets of 5, less often 4, seldom 3 or 2; herbs or woody plants ....**Magnoliopsida** (Dicots), lead 5a

LILIOPSIDA (Monocots)

2a Perianth much reduced and chaffy, or bristly, or fleshy, or wanting. Flowers very small, numerous, and more or less fleshy, aggregated into a spadix that is subtended by a spathe, leaves broad ....**Araceae**, p. 24

2b Perianth well developed, one or both sets of tepals petaloid and more or less showy.

　3a Stamens 3-6; ovary superior or inferior and perianth regular or irregular; seeds with ordinary number and structure.

　　4a Stamens generally 6; ovary generally superior ....**Liliaceae**, p. 24

　　4b Stamens 3; ovary inferior ....**Iridaceae**, p. 36

　3b Stamen 1, adnate to the style; ovary inferior and perianth irregular; seeds numerous ....**Orchidaceae**, p. 38

MAGNOLIOPSIDA (Dicots)
Key to the Groups

5a Petals separate from each other.

　6a Carpels 2 or more, separate, or may be solitary with 1 locule, 1 placenta and 1 stigma ....**Group I**, lead 11a.

　6b Carpels 2 or more and united near the base to form a compound pistil.

　　7a Flowers more or less strongly reduced, unisexual or less often perfect, lacing a perianth, or with very small sepals only, individually inconspicuous, very often some of them borne in catkins or pseudanthia, often appearing before the leaves; plants autotrophic ....**Group II**.

　　7b Flowers generally more normally developed, perfect or less often unisexual, with an evident, often more or less showy perianth; some parasitic plants with usually reduced flowers.

　　　8a Ovary superior, or less than half inferior.

　　　　9a Plants herbaceous or merely suffrutescent at base, or, if occasionally shrubby, then with simple leaves and a single basal ovule ....**Group III**, lead 19a.

　　　　9b Plants woody, not at once simple-leaved and with a single basal ovule ....**Group IV**, lead 33a.

　　　8b Ovary inferior ....**Group V**, lead 36a.

5b Petals united, at least at base.

　10a Ovary superior, or if inferior, then stamens more numerous than corolla lobes ....**Group VI**, lead 49a.

　10b Ovary inferior; stamens alternate with corolla lobes or fewer than corolla lobes ....**Group VII**, lead 62a.

GROUP I

11a Carpels generally 2 or more; herbs except some *rosaceae.*

　12a Stamens attached directly to receptacle, or to lower part of ovary; stipules wanting, or seldom present or small.

　　13a Stamens generally more or less numerous, greater than 10 except in a few species, these with caducous sepals, or more than 5 carpels, or both.

　　　14a Plants aquatic, with large, floating, peltate leaves ....**Nymnphaeaceae** p. 50

　　　14b Plants terrestrial–occasionally aquatic, but not with large, floating, peltate leaves ....**Ranunculaceae** p.50

　　13b Stamens few, not more than 10; sepals generally persistent; carpels 2-5.

　　　15a Carpels 4 or 5; plants succulent ....**Crassulaceae** p. 68

　　　15b Carpels 2 or occasionally 3; plants not notably succulent ....**Saxifragaceae** p. 70

　12b Stamens attached to hypanicum, or attached to outer base of a lobed, perigynous disk.

　　　16a Stamens attached to outer base of a lobed, perigynous disk; leaves exstipule, ternately dissected with broad, flat ultimate segments ....**Paeoniaceae** p. 210

　　　16b Stamens attached to hypanicum; leaves various, generally with stipules, and only seldom ternately dissected ....**Rosaceae** p. 78

11b Carpel solitary, or seemingly so; herbs or woody plants; forms with more than 10 stamens are either aquatic or have anthers opening by terminal uplifting valves.

17a Flowers much reduced, mostly or all unisexual, always individually small and inconspicuous, sometimes with minute sepals, but never with petals; leaves simple, stellate-hairy, annual ....**Euphorbiaceae** p. 104

17b Flowers more or less well developed, perfect or occasionally unisexual, generally with evident sepals or petals or both.

  18a Corolla regular, or wanting; stamens 6-13 (most often 6), distinct; anthers opening by terminal uplifting valves ....**Berberidaceae** p. 62

  18b Corolla irregular, generally papilionaceous (a flower with a banner petal, 2 wing petals and 2 partly connate keel petals); stamens generally 10 (occasionally 9 or 5), all or all but 1 connate by their filaments; anthers opening by longitudinal slits ....**Fabaceae** p. 90

GROUP II

Carpels 2 or more and united; flowers strongly reduced, unisexual or less often perfect, lacking a perianth or with very small sepals only, individually inconspicuous ....**Euphorbiaceae** p. 104

GROUP III

19a Plants aquatic with large, floating leaves, long-pedunculate flowers at the water surface; stamens numerous ....**Nymphaeaceae** p. 50

19b Plants terrestrial to aquatic, neither with large, floating leaves, nor with large, long-pedunculate flowers at the water surface; stamens few to numerous.

  20a Seeds centrospermous (the embryo is elongate, peripheral or nearly so, and generally more or less curved around a generally copious perisperm, or less often spiral or merely folded and the perisperm scanty or none); placentation most often free-central or basal in a unilocular compound ovary.

    21a Sepals fewer than petals, generally 2 (up to 8 in *Lewisia rediviva*, which has 12-18 petals and numerous stamens) ....**Portulacaceae** p. 44

    21b Sepals greater than 2, or the same number as the petals when the flower has petals.

      22a Leaves opposite, rarely alternate or whorled; sepals 4 or 5; petals generally of the same number as the sepals, or occasionally wanting; ovules generally several to numerous on a free-central placenta; herbs ....**Caryophyllaceae** p. 46

      22b Leaves generally alternate, seldom opposite or whorled; sepals 1-6, sometimes in 2 cycles; petals none, unless the inner set of 2 or 3 sepals be so interpreted; ovule solitary on a basal placenta; herbs or occasional shrubs ....**Polygonaceae** p. 40

  20b Seeds not centrospermous; placentation axile to parietal, not free-central or basal in a unilocular ovary.

    23a Plants either with numerous (generally 15) stamens, or with parietal placentation, or both, always chlorophyllous and photosynthetic; some plants with carpels connate below and free above.

      24a Sepals only 2 or 3 ....**Fumariaceae** p. 62

      24b Sepals 4 or more.

        25a Stamens numerous, monadelphous by their filaments, carpels (5) 6 to numerous ....**Malvaceae** p. 106

        25b Stamens few to numerous, but not monadelphous, carpels seldom greater than 5, except in a few *Ericaceae*.

          26a Styles 2 or more, distinct for most or all of their length, or styles wanting and stigmas 2 or more, separate and sessile.

            27a Leaves opposite; stamens numerous, often basally connate into 3-5 groups ....**Hyperiaceae** p. 108

            27b Leaves alternate; stamens few to numerous, not connate into groups.

              28a Carpels exactly as many as the petals, generally 5 or 4; flowers hypogynous; plants succulent ....**Crassulaceae** p. 68

              28b Carpels generally 2, less often 3 (*Lithophragma*) or 4 (*Parnassia*), fewer than the petals; flowers generally perignous, seldom hypogynous, sometimes with other floral parts adnate to lower part of ovary; plants not succulent ....**Saxifragaceae** p. 70

          26b Style 1, with 1 or more stigmas, or stigma 1 and sessile.

            29a Flowers regular or nearly so; carpels 2; stamens seldom less than 6 ....**Brassicaceae** p. 64

            29b Flowers distinctly irregular; carpels 3-4; stamens 5 ....**Violaceae** p. 110

    23b Plants with few (up to 10 or seldom 15) stamens and with axile placentation, or if with distinctly parietal placentation (some *Ericaceae*) then nongreen, lacking chlorophyll.

      30a Styles 2-5, distinct for most or all of their length, or styles wanting and stigmas 2-5, separate, and sessile.

        31a Leaves compound or deeply cleft ....**Geraniaceae** p. 102

        31b Leaves simple, entire or merely toothed ....**Linaceae** p. 104

      30b Styles 1, with 1 or more stigmas.

        32a Carpels 2; stamens 2; petals none ....**Scrophulariaceae** p. 156

        32b Carpels 4 or 5; stamens 5-10; petals present or absent; plants mycotrophic, often lacking chlorophyll ....**Ericaceae** p. 126

GROUP IV (WOODY PLANTS)

33a Leaves compound or palmately lobed ....**Anacardiaceae** p. 106

33b Leaves simple, entire or merely toothed, sometimes much reduced.

34a Ovules and seeds numerous; stamens 5-12, generally 10 ....**Ericaceae** p. 126

34b Ovules and seeds 1-2 per carpel; stamens 3-5.

  35a Stamens alternate with petals ....**Celastraceae** p. 104

  35b Stamens opposite petals ....**Rhamnaceae** p. 106

GROUP V

36a Stamens 6 to numerous.

  37a Leafless, spiny succulents; sepals, petals and stamens numerous ....**Cactaceae** p. 112

  37b Plants leafy, unarmed or occasionally thorny, seldom succulent; sepals and petal seldom greater than 6 each.

    38a Woody plants.

      39a Stigma and style 1; pollen sacs apically elongate, dehiscing by a terminal pore; creeping shrubs ....**Ericaceae** p. 126

      39b Stigmas 2-5; pollen sacs otherwise.

        40a Leaves opposite, exstipules; seeds with abundant endosperm ....**Hydrangeaceae** p. 77

        40b Leaves alternate, generally stipuled; seeds usuallly without endosperm ....**Rosaceae** p. 78

    38b Herbs.

      41a Sepals only 2 or 3 ....**Portulacaceae** p. 44

      41b Sepals 4 or 5 (6).

        42a Styles (or sessile stigmas) 2 or 3; stamens 10 ...   **Saxifragaceae** p. 70

        42b Style 1; stamens 2, 4, 8 or numerous.

          43a Stamens 2-10; sepals and petals generally 4 ....**Onagraceae** p. 114

          43b Stamens numerous; sepals and petals 5 ....**Loasaceae** p. 112

36b Stamens 2-5.

  44a Plants hemiparasitic; ovary unilocular; style 1, sometimes very short ....**Loranthaceae** p. 40

  44b Plants autotrophic; ovary 1 to several-locular, with 1 to several styles.

    45a Leaves opposite; style 1, with capitate to 4-parted stigma.

      46a Woody plants; fleshy fruit; stamens 4 ....**Cornaceae** p. 124

      46b Herbs; dry fruit; stamens 2 or 4 ....**Onagraceae** p. 114

    45b Leaves alternate; styles 2-5.

      47a Ovules and seeds several to numerous; flowers in various sorts of inflorescences, but not in umbels or dense heads.

        48a Shrubs; fruit a berry ....**Grossulariaceae** p. 76

        48b Herbs; fruit a capsule ....**Saxifragaceae** p. 70

      47b Ovules and seeds 1 per carpel; flowers in umbels or dense heads, these often grouped into compound umbels or into racemes, corymbs or panicles ....**Apiaceae** p. 120

GROUP VI

49a Ovaries several (generally 5), connate only below the middle, or free nearly throughout; plants succulent; stamens 10 ....**Crassulaceae** p. 68

49b Ovary 1, of 2 to several carpels, or ovaries 2 but with a common style or stigma; plants not notably succulent; stamens of diverse numbers, sometimes 10.

  50a Placentation free-central or basal in a unilocular ovary.

    51a Corolla regular; stamens at least as many as corolla lobes; plants terrestrial or sometimes aquatic, but not insectivorous.

      52a Stamens as many as the corolla lobes and alternate with them or more often twice as many as the corolla lobes ....**Caryophyllaceae** p. 46

      52b Stamens as many as and opposite the corolla lobes ....**Primulaceae** p. 132

    51b Corolla irregular; stamens 2; plants more or less insectivorous, often aquatic ....**Lentibulariaceae** p. 118

  50b Placentation otherwise.

    52a Stamens twice as many as corolla lobes; anthers dehiscent by terminal pores ....**Ericaceae** p. 126

    52b Stamens as many as corolla lobes and alternate with them, or fewer than corolla lobes; anthers generally dehiscing longitudinally.

      53a Ovules and seeds 4, or fewer by abortion, without endosperm; fruit of 4 more or less distinct or separating 1-seeded nutlets, or the nutlets fewer by abortion; style gynobasic (an enlargement or prolongation of the receptacle).

        54a Stamens 5; corolla regular or seldom somewhat irregular; leaves generally alternate, generally entire; style generally gynobasic ....**Boraginaceae** p. 144

        54b Stamens 4 or 2; corolla slightly to strongly irregular; leaves opposite, entire to more often toothed or cleft; plants generally aromatic ....**Lamiaceae** p. 150

      53b Ovules and seeds either greater than 4, or with endosperm, or both; style never gynobasic and fruit never of 4 nutlets.

        55a Corolla regular or nearly so; stamens isomerous with corolla lobes.

          56a Leaves generally opposite; carpels 2.

57a Carpels united, forming a compound ovary which ripens into a single fruit; plants without milky juice ....**Gentianaceae** p. 134

57b Carpels generally separate, united only by the stigmas and sometimes also the styles, ripening as separate follicles; plants with milky juice.

58a Pollen granular; stamens of ordinary type, separate or merely connivent, only slightly or not at all adnate to stigma, and with an ordinary connective; flowers with a corona ....**Apocynaceae** p. 138

58b Pollen agglutinated into pollinia; stamens of unusual structure, monadelphous and adnate to the stigma, and with an enlarged, ornate connective; flowers with a corona ....**Asclepiadaceae** p. 136

56b Leaves generally alternate.

59a Ovules 2 to numerous per carpel, on parietal or axile placentae, not basal and erect; plants erect to prostrate or occasionally scrambling, but not twining or trailing.

60a Carpels 3; corolla convolute in bud; placentation axile ....**Polemoniaceae** p. 138

60b Carpels 2, very rarely more; aestivation and placentation various.

61a Corolla lobes generally imbricate in bud; style shallowly to deeply cleft; placentation generally parietal ....**Hydrophyllaceae** p. 142

61b Corolla lobes variously folded, contorted, or valvate in bud, but not imbricate; style undivided, with capitate or slightly bilobed stigma; placentation axile ....**Solanaceae** p. 154

59a Ovules 2 per carpel, axile-basal, erect; twining or trailing plants ....**Convolvulaceae** p. 138

55b Corolla more or less strongly irregular; stamens usually fewer than corolla lobes ....**Scrophulariaceae** p. 156

GROUP VII

62a Flowers in various sorts of inflorescences, if in involucral heads then the ovules pendulous, the flowers not blooming in centripetal sequence, and the anthers not connate.

63a Stamens free from corolla, or attached only to its very base; leaves alternate, exstipules ....**Campanulaceae** p. 174

63b Stamens attached to corolla distinctly above its base; leaves opposite or whorled, with or without stipules.

64a Stipules present, cauline, sometimes enlarged and leaflike, the leaves then apparently whorled; corolla regular; stamens as many as corolla lobes; endosperm well developed; herbs ....**Rubiaceae** p. 170

64b Stipules wanting, other features not combined as above.

65a Plants more or less woody stamens generally 5; endosperm well developed; fruits diverse, often fleshy ....**Caprifoliaceae** p. 170

65b Plants herbaceous; stamens 3; endosperm wanting; fruit dry, indehiscent, 1-seeded ....**Valerianaceae** p. 172

62b Flowers borne in dense, involucre, centripetally flower heads; ovary 1-celled, with a solitary, erect ovule; anthers generally connate into a tube around the style, endosperm wanting ....**Asteraceae** p. 174

GLOSSARY

Acaulescent Without a stem.

achene A simple, dry, hard, one-seeded, indehiscent fruit, with seed attached to ovary wall at one point only.

acute Sharp-pointed.

adnate Grown together; applied only to unlike parts.

alternate Referring to the bud or leaf arrangement in which there is a single bud or leaf at each node.

androecium The collective term for the stamens.

angiosperm One of the group of plants magnoliophyta, flowering plants with seeds or ovules enclosed in an ovary.

annual A plant that completes its life cycle within one year and dies.

anther The pollen-bearing organ at the end of a stamen.

axil The upper angle between a leaf or petiole and the stem from which it grows.

axillary Located in or arising from an axil.

Barbed Bearing short, firm, hooked bristles or hairlike projections.

basal Leaves at the base of the plant.

beak A prolonged, slender tip on a thicker organ.

berry A simple fleshy fruit, usually many-seeded and developed from a single pistil.

bi- Latin prefix, meaning two.

biennial A plant which completes its life cycle within two years and dies.

bilabiate Two-lipped.

blade The expanded part of a leaf or petal.

bract A modified leaf, from the axil of which arises a flower or an inflorescence.

bristle A short, coarse, stiff hair.

bulb A short, vertical, underground stem enclosed by many fleshy leaves filled with stored food. An onion is an example.

Calyx The collective term for the sepals; outermost flower whorl.

carpel A floral leaf bearing ovules along the margins, a pistil is composed or one or more carpels.

caudex The persistent, short, upright, often woody, base of an otherwise annual stem from which new stems or leaves arise each year.

cauline Pertaining to the stem.

chlorophyll The characteristic green pigment of plants.

ciliate With a fringe of marginal hairs.

circumboreal Distributed around the globe on a northern latitude.

circumpolar Occurring all the way around the north pole.

clasping A leaf whose base partly or wholly surrounds the stem.

clavate Club or baseball-bat shaped.

cleft A leaf divided about halfway along the midrib.

compound A leaf composed of two or more distinct leaflets.

cordate Heart-shaped with the notch at the base.

cordilleran A chain of mountains occurring and covering much of western North America.

corm A short, vertical, thickened, underground stem in which food is stored.

corolla The collective term for the petals; innermost flower whorl and usually conspicuously colored.

corymb A racemose inflorescence with the lower pedicles progressively longer than the upper pedicles so that all the flowers are at the same level and appear flat-topped.

crenate Scalloped or dentate with rounded teeth.

cyme Usually a convex or flattened inflorescence characterized by having the terminal flower bloom first.

Deciduous Referring to trees and shrubs that lose their leaves in the fall; dying back.

decumbent Reclining or prostrate, with an erect or ascending tip.

decurrent A leaf blade with a wing or margin extending down the petiole on the stem.

dioecious With male and female flowers on separate plants.

disk flowers Small tubular flowers in the center of most members of the sunflower family.

dissected Divided into many small segments.

drupe A simple, fleshy fruit, derived from a single carpel, usually one-seeded, in which the exocarp is thin, the mesocarp fleshy and the endocarp stony.

Elliptic Of, pertaining to, or having the shape of an ellipse.

entire A leaf margin not toothed or otherwise cut.

equitant Astride, as if riding.

Filament The stalk of a stamen.

flora Plants of a particular region or period.

follicle A simple, dry, dehiscent fruit, with one carpel, splitting along one suture.

fruit A ripened ovary or other seed-bearing part of a plant, especially that which is fleshy and edible.

Galea The strongly concave or hood-like upper lip of some bilabiate corollas.

glabrous Smooth, without hairs or glands.

gland A secreting cell or group of cells.

glaucous Covered with a fine wax or powder that produces a whitish or bluish cast to the surface.

globose Sphere-like, round.

Head An inflorescence in which flowers are sessile and grouped closely on a receptacle.

herb A seed plant that does not develop woody tissues, with the stems dying back to the ground at the end of the growing season.

hyaline Clear or translucent.

hypanthium A cup-shaped respectable composed of the fused lower parts of the calyx, corolla and androecium. Sepals, petals and stamens emerge from the edge of the hypanthium.

Imbricate Overlapping, like shingles.

inferior ovary An ovary that is below the petals and stamens or one that is adnate to the calyx.

inflorescence A flower cluster or the arrangement of the flowers on the axis.

involucre A set of bracts beneath an inflorescence.

irregular flower A flower in which one or more members of at least one whorl are of a different form than other members of the same whorl.

Keel A projecting ridge, as in the Leguminosae.

Lanceolate Lance-shaped; long and tapering upward from the middle or below.

ligule The flattened part of the ray corolla in members of the sunflower family.

linear Long and very narrow; line-shaped.

lobe A leaf cut halfway or less to the center with the outer points blunt or rounded.

locule A cavity of the ovary in which ovules occur.

Montane Pertaining to the mountains.

Node An often knob-like marking on a plant stem where a leaf, bud, or stem is attached.

Ob- Greek prefix, meaning in a reverse direction.

oblong Elliptical, blunt at each end, having nearly parallel sides and longer than broad.

obtuse Blunt or rounded.

orbicular Circular in outline.

oval Broadly elliptic.

ovary Enlarged basal portion of the pistil which contains the ovules and becomes the fruit.

ovate Oval or egg-shaped.

ovule A minute structure that, after fertilization, becomes a plant seed.

Palmate Having three or more divisions or lobes and resembling a hand with the fingers extended.

panicle An inflorescence, the main axis of which is branched and whose branches bear loose racemose flower clusters.

parasitic A relationship in which one organism derives nourishment from a living organism of another species without benefiting the other organism.

pedicel The stalk of a single flower in an inflorescence.

peduncle The stalk of an inflorescence or of a solitary flower.

pendulous Hanging loosely or sagging.

perennial A plant that lives from year to year and greater than two years.

perianth The sepals and petals of a flower, collectively.

petal A modified leaf and a member of the corolla; usually colored and serving to attract pollinators.

petiole The stalk of a leaf, attaching it to the stem.

pinnate A compound leaf having similar parts, or leaflets, arranged in sequence along both sides of a petiole, much like a feather.

pistil The seed-bearing reproductive organ of a flower and typically divided into ovary, style and stigma.

plumose Feathery.

pod Any kind of dry, dehiscent fruit.

pome A simple, fleshy fruit where the outer portion is formed by the floral parts that surround the ovary, like an apple.

puberulent Minutely pubescent.

pubescent (pubescence) Covered with short hairs or soft down.

Raceme An inflorescence in which the main axis is elongated and the flowers are borne on pedicels that are about equal in length.

rachis A main axis, such as that of a compound leaf.

ray flowers The ligule or ligulate flower with a strap-shaped corolla as in most members of the sunflower family.

receptacle The end of the flower stalk, bearing the parts of the flower.

rhizome An elongated, creeping, underground modified stem.

rootstock Same as a rhizome.

rosette A cluster of leaves or other organs arranged in a circle or disk, often at the base of a plant.

runner A slender stolon.

Saprophyte A plant that lives on dead or decaying organic matter.

scape An unbranched or leafless stalk arising from the caudex.

sepal One of the leaflike segments of a flower calyx, usually green, but sometimes colored and resembling a petal.

serrate A leaf edge with notched, forward-pointing, toothlike projections.

sessile Attached directly at the base, without a stalk.

shrub A low, woody plant with several stems.

silicle A fruit similar to a silique, but short, not much longer than wide.

silique An elongate capsule in which two valves separate from the seed-bearing partition, usually a fruit characteristic of Brassicaceae (mustards).

simple A leaf all in one piece, not compound.

spathe A large bract or pair of bracts enclosing a flower cluster.

spatulate Spatula-shaped, broad and round at the tip and tapering to the base.

spike An elongate inflorescence of clustered flowers with sessile or subsessile flowers.

spinose A stiff and tough acuminate tip.

spinulose Bearing very small spines.

stalk A stem that supports a plant or plant part.

stamen Generally the male organ of a flower, consisting of the stalk-like filament and the pollen-producing anther.

stellate Star-shaped; radiating in arrangement.

stem The portion of the vascular plant that bears nodes, internodes and leaves.

stigma The part of the pistil that is receptive to pollen.

stipule One of a pair of appendages on each side of the base of certain leaves.

stolon An elongate, creeping stem on the surface of the ground.

strigose Straight, appressed hairs all pointing in more or less the same direction.

style The slender portion of the pistil connecting the stigma and the ovary.

sub- Latin prefix, meaning under, almost, or somewhat.

Taproot A root system with a prominent, stout, vertical root, bearing smaller lateral roots.

tendril A slender, coiling or twining organ that helps support climbing plants.

tepal A sepal or petal, or member of an undifferentiated perianth.

tomentose Covered with tangled or matted, woolly hairs.

toothed Dentate.

trailing Prostrate, but not rooting.

tuber A much-enlarged, short, fleshy underground stem tip, serving in food storage and often in reproduction.

Umbel A racemose inflorescence in which the axis has not elongated, so the flower stalks arise at the same point.

undulate Wavy.

Vascular plant Any plant that has both xylem (principal water and mineral-conducting tissue) and phloem (food-conducting tissue).

vein The vascular portion of a leaf.

viscid Sticky or greasy.

Whorl Three or more structures at a node, as leaves, branches, or floral parts.

wing A thin, flat extension or projection from the margins of a structure.

BIBLIOGRAPHY

Arnberger, Leslie P. 1982. *Flowers of the Southwest Mountains*. Tucson, Arizona: Southwest Parks and Monuments Association.

Burbridge, Joan. 1989. *Wildflowers of the Southern Interior of British Columbia and Adjacent Parts of Washington, Idaho and Montana*. Vancouver, British Columbia: University of British Columbia Press.

Craighead, John J., Frank C. Craighead, Jr. and Ray J. Davis. 1963. *A Field Guide to Rocky Mountain Wildflowers*. Boston, Massachusetts: Houghton Mifflin Company.

Cronquist, Arthur, Arthur H. Holmgren, Noel H. Holmgren and James L. Reveal. 1972. *Intermountain Flora*. Six volumes. New York: Hafner Publishing Company.

Dayton, W.A., and others. 1937. *Range Plant Handbook*. Springfield, Virginia: National Technical Information Service.

Duft, Joseph F., and Robert Moseley. 1989. *Alpine Wildflowers of the Rocky Mountains*. Missoula, Montana: Mountain Press Publishing Company.

Foster, Steven and James A. Duke. 1990. *A Field Guide to Medicinal Plants: Eastern and Central North America*. Boston, Massachusetts: Houghton-Mifflin Company.

Hitchcock, C. Leo and Arthur Cronquist. 1973. *Flora of the Pacific Northwest*. Seattle, Washington: University of Washington Press.

Kirk, Donald R. 1975. *Wild Edible Plants of the Western United States*. Happy Camp, California: Naturegraph Publishers.

Moss, E.H. 1983. *Flora of Alberta*. Second edition revised by J.G. Packer. Toronto, Canada: University of Toronto Press.

Nelson, Ruth Ashton. 1977. *Handbook of Rocky Mountain Plants*. Estes Park, Colorado: Skyland Publishers.

Porslid, A.E. 1979. *Rocky Mountain Wildflowers*. Ottawa, Canada: National Museums of Canada.

Rydberg, P.A. 1922. *Flora of the Rocky Mountains and Adjacent Plains*. New York: Published by the author.

Scotter, George W., and Halle Flygare. 1986. *Wildflowers of the Canadian Rockies*. Edmonton, Alberta: Hurtig Publishers Ltd.

Spellenberg, Richard. 1979. *The Audubon Society Field Guide to North American Wildflowers: Western Region*. New York: Alfred A. Knopf, Inc.

Strickler, Dee. 1990. *Alpine Wildflowers*. Columbia Falls, Montana: The Flower Press.

_____. 1988. *Forest Wildflowers*. Columbia Falls, Montana: The Flower Press.

_____. 1986. *Prairie Wildflowers*. Columbia Falls, Montana: The Flower Press.

Taylor, Ronald J. 1978. *Rocky Mountain Wildflowers: Wildflowers 4*. Beaverton, Oregon: The Touchstone Press.

Taylor, Ronald J. 1992. *Sagebrush Country: A Wildflower Sanctuary*. Missoula, Montana: Mountain Press Publishing Company.

Weber, William A. 1967. *Rocky Mountain Flora*. Boulder, Colorado: University of Colorado Press.

INDEX